Pioneers of the Pacific

Pioneers of the Pacific
Voyages of Exploration, 1787–1810

Nigel Rigby, Pieter van der Merwe
and Glyn Williams

UNIVERSITY OF ALASKA PRESS
FAIRBANKS

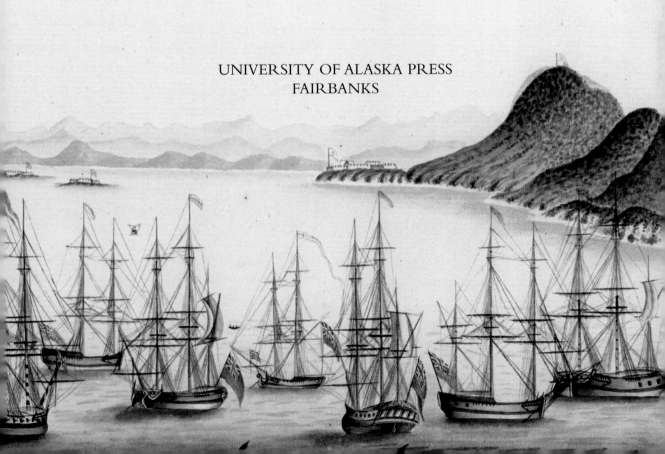

AUTHORS' NOTE

This book is a companion to *Captain Cook in the Pacific* (2002) by the same authors. It aims to introduce the general reader to six of Cook's followers – from Britain, France and Spain – whose voyages both increased Western knowledge of the Pacific and strengthened European involvement in the region. As in the previous volume, the introductory chapter is by Professor Glyn Williams, who, as one of the editors of Malaspina's journals for the new Hakluyt Society edition, has also contributed the chapter on him. Nigel Rigby and Pieter van der Merwe, both of the National Maritime Museum, London, have supplied the others; the former on Lapérouse, Vancouver and Flinders, the latter on Phillip and Bligh.

Text © National Maritime Museum, London, 2005
Illustrations © as listed on page 142

North American edition published and distributed by:
University of Alaska Press P.O. Box 756240 Fairbanks, AK 99775

First published in 2005 by the National Maritime Museum, Greenwich, London, SE10 9NF, UK.

Library of Congress Cataloging-in-Publication Data

Rigby, Nigel.
Pioneers of the Pacific : voyages of exploration, 1787/1810 / Nigel Rigby,
Pieter van der Merwe, and Glyn Williams.
p. cm.
Includes bibliographical references.
ISBN-13: 978-1-889963-76-1
ISBN-10: 1-889963-76-3
1. Oceania—Discovery and exploration. 2. Europe—Colonies—Oceania.
3. Explorers—Oceania—Biography. I. Merwe, Pieter van der. II. Williams, Glyndwr.
III. Title.
DU20.R54 2005
995—dc22   2005020369

Cover images – copyright © National Maritime Museum, London (unless otherwise specified) Front cover (top): 'A General Chart Exhibiting the Discoveries of Captn. James Cook', 1784; (bottom): 'Puget Sound and Mt Rainier from Whitby's Island', by Sarony, Major and Knapp after Stanley, 1860 (PAD0892, not shown in book). Back cover (top): 'The Governor making his best way to the Boat after being wounded by a spear...', by the Port Jackson Painter, 1790 (*Natural History Museum*); (bottom): 'View of Sydney from the East side of the Cove', by John Eyre, *c*.1811. Front flap: '*El fondadero de las corvetas* [*Descubierta and Atrevida*]...' by Ferdinand Brambila, 1790s. (Museo Naval, Madrid). Back flap: 'Islanders and ornaments of Easter Island', by Gaspard Duché du Vancy (*Service historique de la marine, Vincennes*)

Book and jacket design by Mousemat Design Ltd.
Printed and bound in the UK by Cambridge Printing.

CONTENTS

'A General Chart Exhibiting the Discoveries of Captn. James Cook ... with the Tracks of the Ships under his Command ... ', 1784.
Drawn by Lt. Henry Roberts, who sailed on Cook's last two voyages. The *Endeavour*'s track is in red, the second voyage in yellow and the third in gre

CHAPTER ONE

IN THE WAKE OF COOK

'. . . Great Britain . . . must take the lead in reaping
the full advantage of her own discoveries.'
– *Introduction to the official account of Cook's third voyage, 1784*

The death of Captain Cook on a Hawaiian beach in 1779 seemed to close a significant chapter in the story of Europeans in the Pacific. On his three voyages Cook had sketched the main features of the great ocean. On his first he had put more than 5000 miles of previously uncharted coastline on the map, locating Polynesian islands, the larger twin islands of New Zealand and the east coast of Australia. On his second he disposed of the imagined southern continent, reached closer to the South Pole than any other navigator and touched on a host of islands – New Zealand and Tahiti again, and, for the first time Easter Island, the Marquesas, Tonga, New Caledonia and the New Hebrides (Vanuatu). On his third and final voyage he had come across the Sandwich (Hawaiian) Islands in the North Pacific before following the north-west coast of America from Oregon to the Bering Strait in a vain search for a sea passage to the Atlantic. Much remained to be done, but in the way of defining detail rather than in solving major geographical problems.

There were further voyages of exploration to the Pacific in the years after Cook, and not only from Britain. The expedition of Lapérouse, which sailed from Brest in 1785, represented the French response to Cook's voyages. It was one of several important French Pacific voyages over the next decades, for, as a later French navigator, Dumont D'Urville, put it, his countrymen were 'haunted by Cook'. Then, in 1789, a Spanish expedition commanded by Alejandro Malaspina left Cadiz on an ambitious attempt to survey Spain's overseas territories and much else in the Pacific. Although, as Malaspina admitted, his voyage was different from Cook's because 'the habitable portion of the globe could be considered as known', again Cook was the exemplar. In different ways both ventures were ill-fated. Lapérouse disappeared in the south-west

Pacific, and a search expedition by D'Entrecasteaux found no trace of the lost ships. Malaspina survived to complete a voyage of more than five years, but on his return to Spain his political activities led to his disgrace and to the elimination of his voyage from the records. In the first years of the new century Nicolas Baudin commanded a French surveying and scientific expedition intended to complete the charting of the coastline of Australia. It did valuable work in surveying, ethnography and natural history, but its members were divided by political and personal differences. Baudin died at Ile de France (Mauritius) and the expedition was widely regarded as a failure. The contemporaneous British voyage of Matthew Flinders to the same region also experienced more than its fair share of ill luck but his magnificent charts were to be used for many years, and his place names still mark the coastline of the continent soon to be known by the name he used – Australia. It would, it seemed, be left mainly to British seamen to complete and exploit Cook's work in the Pacific, as suggested by John Douglas, the editor of the official account of Cook's last voyage, when he wrote in his Introduction that 'every nation that sends a ship to sea will partake of the benefit [of such accounts]; but Great Britain herself, whose commerce is boundless, must take the lead in reaping the full advantage of her own discoveries'.

Sir Joseph Banks. Watercolour by an unidentified artist, about 1819.

The founding of Botany Bay

Within a few years of the publication in 1784 of the official account the process of exploitation was under way. A fleet sailed for New South Wales to establish the first European settlement in Australia; British and American whalers followed Cook's tracks into far southerly latitudes; William Bligh, master of the *Resolution* on Cook's last voyage, left for Tahiti in the *Bounty* to collect breadfruit for the Caribbean plantations; and British vessels, several commanded by men who had sailed with Cook, were on the north-west coast. Prominent in these ventures was Sir Joseph Banks. The young naturalist who had sailed with Cook on his first voyage was now one of the most influential men in England – President of the Royal Society, patron of the sciences on an international scale, adviser to Cabinet ministers and the promoter of enterprises associated with Cook's discoveries. As James King, who helped to bring the ships home from Cook's third voyage, told him: 'I look up to you as the common center of we discoverers.' Breadfruit from Tahiti, settlement at Botany Bay, the fur trade of the north-west coast of America, the southern whale fishery, all attracted Banks's attention. In the period of national reorganization after the American War of Independence he was a central figure in renewed imperial expansion. The new Pacific voyages were more practical and commercial than scientific but Banks seemed to be involved at every turn.

Banks's time on the *Endeavour* on Cook's first voyage was a turning point in his life, and when in 1779 a government committee enquired as to whether Botany Bay in New South Wales might be among those locations to be considered as a place of transportation for convicts now that the rebellious American colonies were no longer available, Banks was a key witness. No other European ship had reached Australia since the *Endeavour*'s visit, and Cook himself was not available for he was away on his third voyage (and, unknown to anyone in England, already dead). Banks gave a favourable impression of the region: the climate was mild, similar to that of the south of France; the amount of rich soil was limited but it was enough to support a large number of settlers; fish were plentiful; the grass was long and luxuriant; and oxen and sheep would thrive.

With the coming of American independence the matter of where to send the convicts became more urgent, and when in 1785 the government revived its Committee on Transportation, New South Wales reappeared among the possible locations, and again Banks gave evidence. This time he had more to say on the Aboriginal inhabitants. They were few in number; unlike the warlike Maori they were timorous and they seemed to have no political organization. He had no doubt that at Botany Bay they 'would speedily abandon the country to the newcomers'. New South Wales was *terra nullius*, belonging to no one, ready for settlement. Altogether, as Evan Nepean, the official most concerned with the settlement, put it, the region 'appears to be a country peculiarly adapted for a settlement, the lands about it being plentifully supplied with wood and water, the soil rich and fertile, and the shores well stocked with shell and other fish'. Other factors almost certainly played a part in the selection of Botany Bay: the need for a preventive strike to frustrate French initiatives; the advantage of a base situated on the southern, or 'blind' side of the Dutch East Indies; and the hope that the region would provide much-needed naval stores such as timber and flax. Whatever the mix of motives the decision was taken and in May 1787 the eleven ships of the First Fleet sailed from Portsmouth and arrived at Botany Bay in January 1788.

Fur traders in the North Pacific

During the same period that settlement in New South Wales was under consideration, the British were also active in the North Pacific, the scene of Cook's final voyage. Again, Banks was much involved, for he had early sight of the voyage's discoveries as he helped to prepare the journals of the dead navigator and his officers for publication. If Cook's Alaskan explorations in 1778 seemed to have destroyed hopes of a navigable North-West Passage they drew attention to the ease with which seal skins and sea-otter pelts could be obtained along the coast northwards from Cook's landing place at Nootka Sound, on the west coast of Vancouver Island. In the official account of Cook's last voyage, Captain King noted

A sea-otter. Engraving after John Webber, 1784. The official account of Cook's third voyage described how at Nootka Sound in 1778 a sea-otter 'that had just been killed, was purchased from some strangers who came to barter; and of this Mr. Webber made a drawing. It was rather young, weighing only twenty-five pounds; of a shining or glossy black colour; but many of the hairs were tipt with white; gave it a greyish cast at first sight.'

that prime sea-otter pelts, traded for a handful of beads on the north-west coast, fetched as much as $120 at Canton. By the mid-1780s British merchants in India and China were fitting out vessels for the coast, and others from Europe and the United States soon followed. It was, a later writer remarked, as if a new gold coast had been discovered. As increasing numbers of ships reached the coast so relations with the Native peoples – the Haida, Tsimshian, Tlingit and others – became more fraught. The Europeans were outraged by the theft of property from the ships, ranging from nails and trinkets to larger items such as boats and anchors. In turn Native groups resented the newcomers' assumption that resources on shore such as water, wood and game were there for the taking. Both sides had a mutual interest in the trade, but with no common negotiating language misunderstandings were frequent and sometimes ended in violence.

Banks was involved from the beginning in the trading voyages to the north-west coast, primarily through his support of a new enterprise, the King George's Sound Company, headed by Richard Cadman Etches. Banks was, in the words of Richard's brother, John, a leading patron of schemes 'for prosecuting and converting to national utility the discoveries of the late Captain Cook', and the company was known by the name given by Cook to Nootka Sound in 1778 – King George's Sound. The two ships of their first expedition to the north-west coast were commanded by Nathaniel Portlock and George Dixon, both of whom had been on Cook's last voyage. Banks visited the ships as they were fitting out, christened one of them the *Queen Charlotte*, and loaned Portlock a copy of one of Cook's logs. A follow-up venture, again of two ships, was commanded by James Colnett, who had sailed with Cook on his second voyage. All four ships bore names of the royal family: *King George*, *Queen Charlotte*, *Prince of Wales* and *Princess Royal*. In a quite deliberate way the Etches brothers were linking their activities in the North Pacific with royalty, with Cook and Banks and with the pursuit of 'national utility'.

Richard Etches' objective was more ambitious than a series of trading voyages, for Colnett was instructed to establish at least one trading post on the north-west coast, possibly in the newly discovered Queen Charlotte Islands. As Etches explained to Banks: 'Our intention is to adopt a permanent system of Commerce direct from this Country to the N.W. coast and from thence to the Asiatic Coast and Islands.' In a proposal which sought to link British enterprise in the North and South Pacific, Etches suggested that the post or posts might be manned by convicts and guards from Botany Bay. The idea of a British establishment on the north-west coast was strengthened by the reports of discoveries by the trading vessels that seemed to show that Cook's dismissal of the inland straits claimed to have been discovered by Juan de Fuca in 1592 and Bartholomew de Fonte in 1640 might have been premature. Queen Charlotte Sound in latitude 51° north appeared to lead far inland while, even more sensationally, the discovery by William Barkley in 1787 of a strait in latitude 49° north seemed to confirm Juan de Fuca's description of an opening there that led into a great inland sea. Further north, George Dixon had found islands and inlets that matched the reports of Admiral de Fonte's supposed discoveries, but when he reported this to Banks he also drew attention to the fact that the British faced rivals on the coast. The Russians were in Cook Inlet, the Spaniards were just south of Nootka Sound and the French expedition of Lapérouse had traded furs in the region.

By the late 1780s the north-west coast was attracting the attention of geographers, merchants and governments. There, despite the insistence to the contrary of Cook in 1778, it seemed that a strait leading deep into the interior might yet be found. For those enthusiasts eager for a British presence on the north-west coast the region's furs might provide the missing link needed to establish a network of trade encompassing North America, China and Japan. Foremost among the advocates of renewed exploration along the north-west coast was Alexander Dalrymple, hydrographer to the East India Company and an indefatigable publisher of charts and pamphlets. Never a man to think small, Dalrymple proposed a union of the East India Company and the Hudson's Bay Company which, with government support, and using the North-West Passage (if found) to link operations in the Americas and the Pacific, would dominate Europe's trade across a region stretching from the Canadian north to Canton and Bombay. Time was short, he argued, for the Russians were

Engraving of John Meares
published as the frontispiece of his
*Voyages Made in the Years 1788
and 1789, from China to the North
West Coast of America* (1790).

already well established in Alaska while the Spaniards were pressing north from their settlements in Mexico and California.

The Nootka Sound Crisis

Dramatic confirmation of the urgency of the situation came with the Nootka Sound 'incident' in the summer of 1789, when Spanish forces from San Blas seized British ships and property at Nootka Sound, where John Meares had set up a small trading establishment the previous year. Meares was a half-pay lieutenant in the Royal Navy who had first arrived on the north-west coast in 1786 as master of the trading vessel *Nootka*. Unlike other traders on the coast who escaped the rigours of the Alaskan winter by retreating to the Hawaiian Islands, Meares decided to follow the example of the hardy Russian traders by wintering on the coast. In Prince William Sound, as thick snow blanketed the shoreline, the crew were unable to hunt game or take exercise away from the vessel. Confined on board, with little in the way of fresh provisions but a plentiful supply of alcohol to hand, they soon began to show the tell-tale marks of scurvy: bleeding gums, swollen legs and lethargy. In all twenty-four men died (about half the crew), including the ship's surgeon.

Despite this chastening experience, Meares returned to the north-west coast in 1788 in charge of the *Felice Adventurer* and the *Iphigenia Nubiana*, both vessels sailing under nominal Portuguese command and carrying Portuguese colours (to avoid the monopoly rights of the East India Company and the South Sea Company over British vessels trading in the seas east of China). By May of that year, Meares in the *Felice Adventurer* had reached Friendly Cove, visited by Cook ten years earlier, in Nootka Sound. There, according to Meares's later submission, Ma-kwee-na (Maquinna, in the English accounts), the first-ranking chief among the Nuu-chah-nulth people, sold an area of land at the north-east side of the cove to Meares for a pair of pistols. Meares erected a trading hut and began building a small schooner with the help of Chinese carpenters and other workmen on board the two vessels. Looking for trade, Meares sailed south from Nootka as far as the Oregon coast, and on his return north sent his longboat under the first mate, Robert Duffin, to explore the strait discovered by William Barkley two years earlier. How far the longboat penetrated the Strait of Juan de Fuca (as it would soon be known) before Native attack forced it back is not clear, but in his *Voyages…to the North West Coast of America* of 1790 Meares claimed that the strait continued to the east as far as the eye could see and that it might even communicate with Hudson Bay.

The two months spent by Meares on his return to Nootka were eventful ones. He suppressed a mutiny, the *Iphigenia Nubiana* arrived to rejoin the *Felice Adventurer* and his Chinese artificers finished building the little schooner launched under British colours and named the *North West America*. Even more significantly, Maquinna (who had made deadly use of a loan of muskets by the British against local rivals), did 'obedience to us as his lords and sovereigns', or so Meares claimed. There must have been some sort of permission for all the activity going on in the corner of Friendly Cove but whether it carried the implications of Native subordination to the British which Meares placed on it is extremely doubtful. Nor is it likely that the building erected in Friendly Cove was as substantial as described by Meares and hinted at in the engraving in his *Voyages*, for soon after his departure for China by way of Hawaii it was pulled to pieces by the crew of the *Iphigenia Nubiana* before they also left the coast for Hawaii. Since Maquinna and his people had departed for the

Ma kwee-na (Maquinna). Engraving after a drawing by José Cardero from *Relación del viaje hecho por las goletas Sútil y Mexicana* (1802).

interior to spend the winter at Tahsis, the cove was left to the American traders in the *Columbia Rediviva* and the *Lady Washington*.

Far to the north the same summer of 1788 had seen an encounter the repercussions of which were to be felt at Nootka the following year. For twenty years the authorities in New Spain had worried about reports of Russian activities on the Alaskan coast, but none of the several expeditions sent north from Mexico had met Russian traders. Then, in 1788, Esteban José Martínez met Russians in Alaska and reported that they were intending to expand south, possibly as far as Nootka Sound. He recommended, as part of a blocking move, that the Spaniards should occupy Friendly Cove. Russians were not the only threat to traditional Spanish claims to possess the whole of the north-west coast. The French expedition of Lapérouse had investigated Lituya Bay on the Alaskan coast, naming it Port des Français. It was not the entrance to the North-West Passage, as some members of the expedition had hoped, but Lapérouse suggested that it might be a good location for a French trading establishment and with this in mind he purchased an island in the harbour from a local Tlingit chief. The increasing number of British and American traders arriving to exploit the sea-otter trade sent further warning signals to the nervous Spanish authorities in Mexico.

Martínez was mistaken in thinking that the Russians had any designs on Nootka Sound, but in the spring of 1789 he sailed from San Blas bound for Nootka with what, in north-west coast terms, was a powerful force of two ships carrying forty-two cannon and two hundred men. At the same time British trading vessels, including the tiny *North West America*, were heading for Nootka from the Hawaiian Islands and China. Given Martínez's impulsive temperament, confrontation was inevitable. In May the *Iphigenia* and her crew were detained and then released, but in early June the *North West America* was seized and taken into the Spanish service. The real crisis came with the arrival of James Colnett in the *Argonaut*, carrying Chinese workmen who were to build boats and a trading post (to be named Fort Pitt) at Nootka. The arrest of the *Argonaut* and its crew, followed by the seizure of another Etches vessel, the *Princess Royal*, was the prelude to scenes of high drama as Martínez and Colnett quarrelled, sometimes sword in hand. The Spaniard's fondness for alcohol did not help matters, while Colnett's unstable character resulted in at least one attempted suicide. The tension apparent in the circumstances was shown when a Spanish crew member shot dead Maquinna's associate chief, Callicum, when he sought to intervene in a dispute. Eventually, orders came from San Blas, where the authorities had heard nothing of these events, to evacuate Nootka, and in October Martínez sailed south with his prisoners. The American vessels had already left while Maquinna's people had retreated inland to Tahsis. As winter closed in, Friendly Cove was deserted; its silent waters gave no indication of the international storm that was brewing.

The first news of the events at Nootka Sound reached Britain in early

'The Launch of the *North West America* at Nootka Sound. Being the first Vessel that was ever built in that part of the Globe', in *Voyages*, by John Meares (1790). A dramatic rendering of the launch of 20 September 1788, with British flags flying on both the schooner and Meares's building. The cliff-like heights of Friendly Cove shown here should be compared with the more accurate drawing made by Henry Humphrys in 1792 (see p. 17).

1790 by way of its diplomats in Spain. The government's first reaction was to secure an apology from Spain together with recognition of British rights to trade and settle in areas not actually occupied by Spain. This was accompanied by preparations to send a naval expedition to the north-west coast by way of New South Wales, commanded by Henry Roberts, who had been with Cook on his last voyage. His draft instructions reveal the various motives at work. Roberts was to find out what had actually happened at Nootka in the summer of 1789 (the government's priority), explore the coast (as Dalrymple was urging) and put thirty or so Marines, overseers and convicts from Sydney ashore in the Queen Charlotte Islands where they would establish a settlement (the scheme promoted by Banks and Etches). In late April 1790 the expedition was cancelled, for Meares had arrived in England and his evidence put the whole matter on a different and more alarming footing. He claimed that in his dealings on the north-west coast he had acted as an officer in the Royal Navy; that as such he had bought land at Nootka and taken possession of it in the King's name, and that he had secured recognition of British overlordship from Maquinna. If Meares was right a British settlement had already been established on the north-west coast, although the actual building seemed to have been dismantled before the Spanish arrival. What had been seen as the manhandling of British traders turned into an insult to the British crown, and an obscure scuffle became a confrontation in which the whole question of trading and territorial rights on the north-west coast and beyond was at stake. As Henry Dundas, the British minister most involved in the affair, told the House of Commons, 'We are not contending for a few miles, but a large world', for he had in mind a release from international restrictions that would benefit British traders on a massive scale. Or, as Etches remarked to Banks, it was not simply a case of 'the immediate property seized' at Nootka but of 'great and certain prospects' in trade and discovery.

Spurred on by bellicose public opinion, the British government mobilized the fleet and prepared for war. Spain, preparing to fight yet another rearguard action in defence of her traditional claims in America, realized that France, formally her ally, was in no position to offer help at a time of revolution and upheaval within the country. By the terms of the Nootka Sound Convention signed in October 1790 Spain conceded the main points at issue by agreeing to return the land and property seized the previous summer, and allowing free access and trade along those parts of the north-west coast not occupied by Spain – in effect the whole coast. British naval ships would be sent to the region under the command of George Vancouver, who had been chosen as first lieutenant to Henry Roberts on the expedition planned earlier in the year. He was given two tasks: to receive restitution of the land and property at Nootka, and to explore the coast as far north as latitude 60° north to determine, once and for all, whether there was a navigable North-West Passage in temperate latitudes. This survey would be all the more important because of Spain's abandonment of its exclusive claim to the north-west coast. The task took

Vancouver and his crews three seasons of wearisome work in open boats, often in poor weather, and with the threat of Native attack always present. At the end, Vancouver hinted at his attitude to the main objective of the survey when he remarked on the merriment among his crew 'in consequence of our having sailed from old England on the *first of April*, for the purpose of discovering a north-west passage', and summed up his approach when he stated that his 'discovery that no such communication does exist has been zealously pursued, and with a degree of minuteness far exceeding the letter of my commission or instructions'.

On the diplomatic issue Vancouver met difficulties in his negotiations at Nootka, where the Spaniards had established a fort and other buildings much more impressive than Meares's shanty hut. At a loss in his dealings with the affable but firm Spanish representative, Francisco de la Bodega y Quadra, Vancouver broke off negotiations, much to the irritation of the British government. Vancouver, far distant in the North Pacific, was not to know that Britain and Spain were now allies against Revolutionary France, and he received no further instructions or information from home. The incident at Nootka was fading into obscurity and further agreements between the two governments laid down that after a symbolic restitution there would be a mutual abandonment. This was carried out in 1795 and, as the Spanish and British commissioners sailed away (in a Spanish ship), Maquinna's people began demolishing the Spanish fortifications in their search for nails and ironwork. In the long term the nation that benefited most from the Spanish retreat at Nootka was the United States, which had not been involved in the negotiations at all. There were fewer British ships on the coast after Vancouver's visit and the sea-otter trade was in decline. Soon the region would be dominated by American fur traders, who, in the new century, also began to arrive overland as spearheads of the American drive towards the Pacific.

'Friendly Cove, Nootka Sound'. Engraving in George Vancouver's *A Voyage of Discovery to the North Pacific Ocean* (1798), based on a drawing by Midshipman Henry Humphrys during Vancouver's stay at Nootka Sound in 1792. Spanish buildings are shown on the left, while on the far right the letters 'A' and 'B' near the shore indicate the extent of land in dispute between Britain and Spain.

Perhaps even more disappointing to Vancouver than London's failure to keep in touch with him over the details of the Nootka transaction was the government's lack of response to his achievement – as he regarded it – in negotiating the cession in February 1794 of the Hawaiian Islands to Britain. The islands afforded the essential wintering base for ships trading on the north-west coast, where Meares's experience in 1786–87 had shown the dangers of wintering. Oddly, although Vancouver left a letter in Hawaii explaining to the masters of all vessels which called there that Kamehameha and his chiefs had 'unanimously acknowledged themselves subject to the British crown', he seems never to have informed the government at home of what he had done – or if he did the letter has not survived (his last known letter to the Admiralty, from Hawaii, was written on 8 February 1794, several weeks before the act of cession). The affair was set out in detail in Vancouver's account of his voyage, published in 1798, but his description ended on a rather deflating note as he pondered 'whether this addition to the empire will ever be of any importance to Great Britain, or whether the surrender of the island will ever be attended with any additional happiness to its people, time alone must determine'. In the event there was no follow-up from the government. Perhaps it suspected that Vancouver's act of cession was of doubtful validity, or it may be that the status of a handful of remote islands in the Pacific seemed a marginal matter as the pressures of all-out war dominated British government thinking.

Whalers, traders and missionaries
The Nootka Sound Convention also had implications for British enterprise in the South Pacific. By the second half of the eighteenth century the Greenland whale fishery could not meet the growing demand for oil and Cook's charting of the Pacific encouraged both British and American whalers to sail to far southerly latitudes in pursuit of the sperm whale. Among the vessels of the First Fleet were several whalers under charter to the government, and, as the fleet approached Botany Bay, one of the captains reported sighting more whales in a single day than he had seen off the coast of Brazil in six years. For the British (but not the American) whalers there was a problem, since they were sailing into seas which lay within the monopoly rights of the East India Company and the South Sea Company. Drawn-out negotiations between the government and the chartered companies partly, though not entirely, resolved the difficulty. A different sort of obstacle was the lack of bases in the southern oceans where the whalers and sealers could repair their vessels and refresh their crews. Again, British rather than American seamen suffered more from Spanish intractability. The refusal to allow two British whalers to enter a Spanish harbour in Patagonia in April 1789 showed the nature of the problem, which became more acute every year as increasing numbers of British whalers (more than fifty in 1791) entered the Pacific, many of them by way of Cape Horn. Without a friendly port some of the whalers were at sea for up to a year and their crews suffered heavy losses, especially from scurvy.

While negotiations were taking place on the Nootka dispute the British government made it clear that among its demands was the freedom of British subjects to hunt whales in any part of the Pacific, and to land for repairs and refreshments in any unoccupied harbour. The first Nootka Sound Convention of 1790 formalized this with its proviso that the coasts of Spanish America should be accessible to non-Spanish trade and settlement except within thirty miles of an existing settlement. This had opened to access virtually all the north-west coast and possibly some of the uninhabited islands off the Pacific coast of South America, one of which might provide the base the whalers were seeking. A problem was the lack of reliable surveys of those waters, so in 1792 the *Rattler* commanded by James Colnett of Nootka fame sailed on a joint government–private expedition to examine islands off the coast from Chile to Mexico.

By the time of Colnett's return in 1794 with an enthusiastic report on the Galápagos Islands the difficulty had been resolved in a different way, since the whalers were using New Zealand, Hawaii and, especially, Sydney, as supply places. After surviving its first difficult years the infant colony in New South Wales had made great strides in developing an agricultural and trading economy. By the end of the century Sydney harbour was a base not only for whalers but for trading vessels, some heading for China and India, others for the islands of Polynesia where they would trade for pork, sandalwood and later copra and coconut fibre. In the nineteenth century the once-dreaded convict settlement of Botany Bay had grown into the bustling port-city of Sydney. Within a generation

'View of Sydney from the East Side of the Cove', by John Eyre, in D. D. Mann's *The Present Picture of New South Wales* (1811), gives a good impression of how the port looked in about 1800.

of Cook's death the Pacific was criss-crossed by the tracks of the traders, whalers and sealers. In terms of both volume and value the Pacific trade was still slight compared with that of the North Atlantic or the Indian Ocean, but almost 300 years after Magellan's voyage the great ocean had at last been brought within Europe's sight.

As the novelty of the ecstatic discoveries of Cook's day faded, so did the earlier philosophical assumptions that Britain could learn much from the Pacific. The South Seas retained their allure but as a remote haven for the few, far removed from the conventions of civilized society. The islands themselves were changing fast. George Vancouver, who had visited Tahiti with Cook on his second and third voyages, noted with foreboding on his voyage of the 1790s the differences in Tahitian custom. European implements and supplies were now in common use, to such an extent that the islanders had abandoned 'their former tools and manufactures, which are now growing fast out of use, and, I may add, equally out of remembrance'. This was not necessarily a one-sided matter, to be deplored regardless of circumstances as some sort of 'fatal impact'. Despite the episodes of violence and abuse, the islanders were usually co-operative, often eager, partners in the trading exchanges. Even so, many of the whalers and traders were the rejects of society. Their uncontrolled activities did lasting harm and the alcohol, firearms and disease which accompanied them made a deadly combination. No government accepted responsibility for the actions of its subjects in the islands and the only resistance came from the missionaries, committed to protecting those whose souls might be saved. A sermon delivered by Thomas Haweis to the London Missionary Society soon after its founding in 1795 spoke of the 'enchanting scenes' of Polynesia, but in a melodramatic passage warned his congregation that there 'savage nature still feasts on the flesh of its prisoners – appeases its Gods with human sacrifices – whole societies of men and women live promiscuously, and murder every infant born among them'. The next year the missionary vessel *Duff* left for Tahiti, and soon the accounts of the explorers were supplemented by the reports of devoted missionaries whose task it was to rescue the Pacific islanders from eternal hell-fire. Unfortunately, the effects of this well-intentioned intervention were no less destructive of indigenous cultures and societies.

There is little likelihood that Cook, who has come down to us as an essentially secular person, ever remotely considered that missionaries might be sent to the islands before the end of the century. But then it would have taken a considerable stretch of the imagination for him to visualize the departure from Portsmouth of a fleet of eleven ships carrying convicts to Botany Bay, or to anticipate the clash of great powers over trading rights in Nootka Sound. It was perhaps Georg Forster, who had sailed with Cook on the second voyage, who foresaw most clearly the results of the explorer's surveys when he wrote, 'What Cook has added to the mass of our knowledge is such that it will strike deep roots and long have the most decisive influence on the activities of men.'

The Cession of Matavai to Captain James Wilson, by Robert Smirke RA. This celebrated painting shows a ceremonial meeting of Tahitian priests and chiefs, missionaries, and ship's officers, held soon after the arrival of the missionary vessel *Duff* at Tahiti in March 1797. Like many such ceremonies, it represented not a cession of land, as assumed by the visitors, but a conditional offer of help and hospitality.

CHAPTER TWO

'GENTLEMAN, SCHOLAR AND SEAMAN': ARTHUR PHILLIP AND AUSTRALIA

'Governor Phillip is a good Man, remember me
kindly to him . . .'
– Rear-Admiral Sir Horatio Nelson to his wife, 17 April 1798

*C*ook's exploration and charting of the eastern Australian coast in 1770 was a signal achievement but one without immediate practical consequence. For nearly twenty years there were no further European landings in the vast territory that he named New South Wales, whose Aboriginal inhabitants were briefly left to its immemorially uncontested occupation.

British attention was instead diverted, from 1775, by the American War of Independence which, from 1778, became a European seaborne conflict as France, Spain and the Dutch in turn backed the American rebels. One consequence of their revolt was to stop the transportation of about 1000 British convicts a year, most to Virginia and Maryland, as cheap plantation labour. But this suspension did not end the legal sentence of transportation – seven years, fourteen or life – and, while considering alternative destinations, the British government instituted a system of prison hulks, in which transportees were held and employed in heavy dockyard and river work. Run by the contractor Duncan Campbell, the hulks were effective but had limited capacity, and London was soon being assailed by local complaints about the costs of the overflow backing up in civic jails. Among new places of exile considered, three suggested in 1784 and 1785 combined both distance and utility.

Two convict colonies in southern Africa, proposed as staging posts on the route to India, quickly gave way for practical reasons to the third, on which Cook and Banks had already reported. This was Botany Bay, Cook's first landing point in south-eastern Australia, at the end of a long but straightforward voyage before the prevailing westerlies from the Cape of Good Hope. It also seemed to offer other advantages, more vaunted than real: as a base against French threats in the Indian Ocean, against

Dutch interests in the East Indies or the Spaniards in the Philippines and even on the western American coasts. Occupation of New South Wales would also deny this to the French and possibly offer new natural resources: Cook had already indicated the naval potential of Norfolk Island pine and New Zealand flax.

The costs and outline of the scheme were approved in August 1786 but a voyage to establish a convict colony would require an exceptional leader and, thereafter, resident governor. Since the political responsibility fell principally within the remit of the Home Secretary, Lord Sydney, it was he – advised by his more able under-secretary, Evan Nepean – who chose an obscure forty-seven-year-old naval captain called Arthur Phillip. That this choice was against the preference of the formidable Lord Howe, First Lord of the Admiralty, itself suggests unusual qualifications in the nominee.

Captain Arthur Phillip, by Francis Wheatley, 1786. Commissioned just before Phillip went to Australia by Elizabeth, widow of his relative and early naval patron Captain Michael Everitt. She later gave it to Phillip's second wife.

Before Australia

Few personal documents relating to Phillip survive. Given his own lack of bravura and the secret work in which he was sometimes involved, this helps to make him one of the least-known founders of any modern state – as he was of Australia. It was also characteristic that, like Cook, he succeeded by doing nothing more romantic than carrying out his instructions in a highly competent manner.

Arthur Phillip was born in St Olave's parish in the City of London on 11 October 1738. His father, Jacob, was a German from Frankfurt who taught languages. His mother, Elizabeth, was already a widow from her first marriage to a seaman called John Herbert and had a useful connection in a cousin, Michael Everitt, a naval captain. The couple probably married in 1736, when a daughter, Rebecca, was born, but after a few years of modest prosperity Jacob seems to have been dead by 1751. In June that year Arthur was admitted to the Greenwich Hospital School for the sons of poor seamen. While his mother's Everitt connection may have helped, its records give Jacob's occupation as both a 'steward' and an 'able seaman'. Whether this was before his marriage or in the 1740s is unknown but the Marquis of Lavradio, Portuguese Viceroy of Brazil, later reported that Arthur first went to sea in the Navy at the age of nine and it might have been briefly with his father. Jacob's principal legacy to his twelve-year-old son was fluency in spoken and written German, 'an excellent grounding in Latin … and some knowledge of French', which his later career enabled him to perfect. Lavradio said that he spoke six languages: he learnt Portuguese in Brazil and circumstances suggest that he also had Spanish. The sixth, assuming Latin did not count, is uncertain.

In 1753, the Revd Francis Swinden, the headmaster at Greenwich, was able to write at the end of his pupil's brief schooling there: 'Arthur Phillip is noted for his diplomacy [and] mildness. [He is] nervously active, unassuming, reasonable, business-like to the smallest degree in everything he undertakes, always seeking perfection.' Similar characteristics – of reserve, honesty, educated principle and frank but respectful reasonableness, not least in contrast with other English 'excesses of temper' – were to be echoed in the praise he received from the Viceroy. Swinden would also have been pleased to hear his old pupil described much later as a combination of 'the Gentleman, the scholar and the seaman'.

All Greenwich boys were educated for sea careers and on 1 December 1753 Phillip was apprenticed to William Redhead, master of the Arctic whaler *Fortune* of London, which, like many others, also traded in other cargoes out of season. Between April and July 1754 he made his first whaling voyage, followed by one in August to the Mediterranean before

A boy of the Greenwich Hospital School, about 1725, as represented by James Thornhill in the vestibule of the Painted Hall of what is now the Old Royal Naval College, Greenwich.

returning to London via Rotterdam in April 1755. Another Arctic voyage immediately ensued, returning in July, when Phillip's apprenticeship to Redhead prematurely ended. Exactly why is unknown, but the initial skirmishes of the Seven Years War with France (1756–63) were then beginning and, at a rather earlier age than Cook before him, Phillip must have seen greater opportunities in a naval career. He embarked on this in the traditional role for officers of 'captain's servant' under his relative Captain Everitt in the *Buckingham*, 68 guns, flagship of Vice-Admiral Temple West in the Channel Squadron. He joined at Plymouth six days after his seventeenth birthday and by mid-November had taken part in the capture and burning of a French 74-gun ship. The following year in the Mediterranean the *Buckingham* shared in the incompetent fleet action with the French off Minorca that led to Britain's loss of that island. Phillip sent his sister an indignant account of it and the 'Cowardice of Admiral Byng' – subsequently court-martialled and shot.

On Everitt's recall Phillip remained in other ships in the Mediterranean (including, briefly, as a captain's clerk) until rejoining him and West as a midshipman in the 98-gun *Neptune* at Portsmouth early in 1757. That July he was hit by one of the bouts of periodic ill health that dogged his life and went ashore, only definitely returning to sea in mid-1759 and rejoining Everitt in the *Stirling Castle* in February 1760. She sailed for the Leeward Islands in September and on 7 June 1761 he was appointed the ship's fourth lieutenant by the local commodore. As such he was involved in Admiral Rodney's capture of Martinique from the French

Greenland whalers in the Arctic; detail from a painting by Charles Brooking (1723–59). The *Fortune*, in which Phillip first sailed, was probably very similar to the English whaler shown.

early in 1762, and in the great amphibious expedition later that year that briefly took Havana, Cuba, from the Spanish. Phillip seems to have shown his good qualities there and came to the notice of Captain Augustus Hervey, whose patronage proved important to him two years later. The Admiralty confirmed his commission when he returned to England in March 1763, but the onset of peace that year saw him discharged on half-pay, albeit with £130 of Havana prize-money to ease the transition.

In July 1763 Phillip married Mrs Charlotte Denison, sixteen years older and the well-off widow of a London cloth merchant. Given his new wife's background and his own later interests he may have been involved in some aspect of trade for the next two years but, probably by the end of 1765, they had bought a small farm near Lyndhurst in Hampshire. Gentlemanly management of it was to be valuable experience for Phillip but unfortunately and for unknown reasons his marriage failed and he sought a legal separation. By mid-1769 he was on his own again and in debt to his wife, who had retained legal control of her own property. For the next four years he appears to have oscillated between two long periods of official leave 'for the benefit of his health' in France and the Low Countries, with eight months of home naval service, primarily in the *Egmont*, in 1770–71.

It seems fairly certain that he earned enough money abroad to settle his debts to Charlotte, possibly by acting as an agent in the cloth trade on behalf of London friends. He may also have pursued engineering and military studies in Europe, in which he had acquired an unusual theoretical knowledge by the 1770s. Sometime before 1778 he had assessed the French naval base at Toulon, so he may have volunteered, or been asked for, intelligence about a fleet fitting out there early in 1773. Phillip's portraits show his mild, unremarkable appearance: along with discretion, thoroughness and a command of languages, unobtrusiveness is a valuable asset to a spy.

On return to peacetime England in 1774, Phillip adopted a fairly common option for unemployed but ambitious officers: he enlisted abroad. Portugal and Spain were then in dispute over territory on the northern side of the River Plate estuary in what is now Uruguay and southern Brazil. Here the Portuguese had established a fortified outpost at Colonia do Sacramento, across the Plate from Buenos Aires. A Spanish assault on it in 1773 was repulsed by the Viceroy, Lavradio, who also sought reinforcements from home. Portugal requested naval help from Britain, her oldest ally, which was limited to allowing the recruitment of a few unemployed naval officers. The British had long sought to penetrate Spain's jealously guarded South American trade and Hervey, now at the Admiralty, knew that information on those coasts could prove valuable. The only volunteer he unreservedly recommended was Lieutenant Phillip, praising his experience, knowledge, judgement and good French (then the international language). That he would acquire information of possible use for London would have been tacitly understood.

Phillip obtained generous terms from the Portuguese, including the rank of a captain in their navy. He left for Lisbon in December 1774 and arrived at Rio on 5 April 1775. There he swiftly confirmed his good qualities with the Viceroy, not least in contrast to Robert M'Douall, the blustering British officer who was already commodore of the local naval forces. Lavradio gave him independent command of the *Nossa Senhora do Pilar*, a merchantman under conversion to a 26-gun frigate. In her he put new fibre into the defence of Portuguese interests on the disputed coast and at Colonia, including in command of a small squadron there. When a large Spanish force arrived off Lavradio's southern naval base of Santa Catarina Island early in 1777, M'Douall's irresolution led to its unresisting surrender, with only one Portuguese captain and Phillip demurring. They probably both felt their honour redeemed by their sharp attack in April on the superior Spanish *San Augustin*, 70 guns, which then surrendered to the squadron. Phillip's reward was to take command of her until peace was concluded in April 1778, when Spain gained Colonia in exchange for the return of Santa Catarina and recognizing Portuguese sovereignty in southern Brazil.

Phillip gained much else from his Brazilian service. Through Lavradio's friendship he enjoyed a high level of social entrée, including to local scientific circles, and within a year he was writing and speaking fluent Portuguese. He charted or obtained charts of the coast as part of his official duties, and learnt about local settlements and defences, agriculture and produce. His experience at Colonia also taught him the hardships of sustaining an isolated outpost with an unwilling population and he may have been the first Englishman to enter the forbidden interior zone of Minas Gerais to observe gold and diamond mining, which hardened a distaste for slavery that he probably first acquired in the West Indies. Lavradio saw him leave with regret, sending him back to Lisbon in mid-1778 with a report praising his judgement, integrity, tact and sometimes high-handed bravery. With the American War now in full swing, Phillip wanted to return to the Royal Navy: Lisbon, echoing Lavradio's praise of his 'zeal and honour', could only regretfully comply.

On arriving home in September, he lost his Portuguese rank of captain but was appointed first lieutenant of the 74-gun *Alexander* in the Channel squadron and in September 1779 raised to master and commander of a fireship. When this did not go into service he substituted for absent captains in two larger vessels but his movements were otherwise shadowy until late 1781, when he was finally made post-captain in the frigate *Ariadne* and sent to collect Hanoverian troops from the Elbe. A reputation for dealing with unusual situations and his command of German probably recommended him, and both came into play when *Ariadne* was trapped by ice and had to be secured for winter there, only returning in spring 1782.

More significant at this time was his likely role as an adviser on naval policy in South America. It brought him into direct contact with Lord Sandwich, First Lord of the Admiralty, and others who were to be important to him, including Evan Nepean – later secretary in both Home Office and Admiralty – and Nepean's master in the former, Thomas Townshend, later Lord Sydney. Spanish and Dutch alliance with the American rebels in 1779–80 was then prompting a series of complex expeditionary proposals. They included revived plans for action against the Spanish in South America, seizure of the Cape of Good Hope from the Dutch and the ongoing need to safeguard British interests in India. Commodore George Johnstone's expedition to take the Cape sailed in 1781, with Plate operations from there a later possibility, but the plan collapsed when the French intercepted him in a drawn action off the Azores.

In all this it is fairly clear that Phillip supplied advice to Sandwich and the government, and copies of his South American charts. Early in 1781, he may also have commanded a merchant ship taking Portuguese army recruits (including convicts) to Rio. If so his real purpose would have been to gather intelligence for anti-Spanish moves and success in doing so might help to explain his promotion to post-captain that autumn. In December 1782 he was appointed captain of the 64-gun *Europe* in a squadron sent to reinforce Admiral Sir Edward Hughes in India but arrived at Madras alone, all the other ships having been forced back by bad weather. Phillip himself had to put into Rio for repairs, where he received 'every possible mark of respect and attention', but his stay in India was short. In October 1783 Hughes ordered him home in Commodore Sir Richard King's squadron which reached Cape Town early in December, storm-damaged and heavily afflicted with scurvy. When Phillip was sent to ask permission to land the sick the Dutch at first refused, claiming they had no confirmation of a recent truce with England, and it was an indication of Phillip's standing that King sent him home in advance with official protests and Hughes's Indian despatches.

Arriving in April 1784 he again asked for a year's leave, from mid-October, to attend to private affairs in Grenoble, on this occasion certainly cover for a peacetime spying mission. At the Home Office Nepean paid him £150 from secret funds in November to check reports of a French warship-building programme at Toulon. Phillip confirmed this was under way and, tellingly, that the arsenal there was 'in very good Order and very superior to what it was when I saw it before the War'. He returned to England in October 1785 but left again in December for another year's official absence to Hyères, just west of Toulon. Since Nepean authorized a second related payment to him of £160 there is no doubt that his undercover work continued there, whatever else he might have been doing for his London merchant friends.

'The City of St Sebastian', from Phillip's carefully checked copy of the large-scale Portuguese chart (c. 1776) of the harbour of Rio de Janeiro that he brought home from his service in Brazil. This detail shows the historic core of modern Rio.

'The First Fleet'

By 1786, Phillip was a man of wide experience in distant voyages, foreign service, diplomacy and languages, in financial matters of a commercial as well as an official nature, and the observation of Portuguese, Spanish and Dutch colonial practice (the last at the Cape) in agriculture and defence. He had also advanced from modest origins on his steadiness, proven courage and talent for accomplishing unusual tasks. All these factors probably underlay his nomination for the Botany Bay project.

His response was an imaginative and detailed paper on how the voyage and what followed should be conducted for the health and welfare of the convicts, and how reform, work and the success of the colony would open up opportunities for them. He considered the necessary supplies, equipment, plants, seeds and breeding animals; the required laws, punishments and incentives, including making private grants of cultivable land to both transportees on expiration of their sentences and the Marine force sent as their guards. He addressed the protection and segregation of women convicts but the probable need to condone a degree of prostitution, while also wishing to encourage stable marriages, either among the transportees or with Polynesians (the last also applying to the Marines). He was also determined to encourage good relations with the Aborigines, to promote their enlightened 'civilization' and to protect them under the same English laws that governed the colony. He included the very specific tenet 'That there can be no Slavery in a Free Land – and consequently no Slaves', a provision which was rapidly abrogated by his military successors in New South Wales in their treatment of later transportees. Further complex legal arrangements were concluded to allow him to exercise law as civil governor, under a number of technically separate jurisdictions.

Beyond such principles, Phillip immersed himself in all the practical details of fitting ships, appointing officers – including former shipmates like Phillip Gidley King from *Ariadne* and *Europe*. He also exerted pressure to obtain 'Provisions and accommodations better than any Set of Transports' than one harassed Navy Board colleague had ever seen, although much with which he was supplied proved inadequate. His one failure was to be formally appointed commodore by the Navy although he was generally referred to as such, and was given a second captain in John Hunter for his 'flagship'. Overall and with many delays the process took nine months, with Phillip and Nepean ensuring that orders were issued by personally visiting all the heads of department concerned and waiting until they were, as Cook had done.

For the voyage the Navy Board refitted the 540-ton naval transport *Berwick*, now renamed *Sirius*, and the 175-ton brig *Supply*, and contracted nine civilian ships. The *Alexander*, *Scarborough*, *Charlotte*, *Friendship*, *Lady Penrhyn* and *Prince of Wales* were convict transports. The first two took men only, the third and fourth men and women and the last two women, except for one man in the *Prince*. The last ship was only added late in the day, when the number of female transportees was increased, and to carry extra baggage and stores. The *Fishburn*, *Golden Grove* and *Borrowdale* were storeships, while the *Charlotte* and *Lady Penrhyn* were chartered by the East India Company to reduce costs by collecting tea from China as a return cargo.

At 114 feet long and 452 tons, the *Alexander*, built in 1783, was the largest transport, carrying 195 male prisoners confined in an unlit and underventilated 'tween deck of only 4 foot 5 inch clearance. (The 430-ton *Scarborough* carried even more, at 208.) *Alexander* was also the dirtiest, delaying departure when typhus broke out on board. This was quickly contained but the ship remained dirty and unhealthy until Phillip later insisted the master have her regularly pumped and cleansed. The typhus outbreak at least gave Phillip late leverage to gain the quantity of fresh provisions that he wanted, although he still sailed short of clothes for female convicts and without adequate musket balls to contain a determined rebellion. Although it was suggested these might follow in the *Bounty* when she sailed for Tahiti, Phillip was able to make up this deficiency and others at Rio and the 'First Fleet' of Australia's European history eventually sailed from Portsmouth on 13 May 1787. With Phillip in *Sirius* went the Kendall chronometer ('K1') used by Cook on his last two voyages.

The fleet's convict cargo – 546 men and 190 women by one modern count, though the figures vary – comprised neither the greatest villains of Georgian society nor political prisoners, albeit some of them were educated. Of the 262 whose ages are known five were under fifteen, 234 between sixteen and forty-five and thirteen older. Largely from London, they were a harvest of failure and destitution, most sentenced for crimes against property. This was sometimes serious – including theft from employers and burglary (ninety-three cases), highway robbery (seventy-one), sheep and cattle stealing (forty-four) and violent mugging (thirty-one). There were also a few dealers in stolen goods, swindlers and forgers, but the majority of known crimes (431 out of 733) were minor thefts, often through necessity: a hen or two, some cheese or bacon, a shilling's worth of butter in one case. A starving black West Indian called Thomas Chaddick took some cucumbers from a garden; John Hudson, a nine-year-old chimney sweep, some clothes and a pistol; Elizabeth Hayward aged thirteen, a clogmaker, clothing to the value of seven shillings. These were the youngest. Dorothy Handland, a perjured rag dealer, was the oldest: aged eighty-two she would also be Australia's first recorded suicide. Most were ill-suited as colonial pioneers with only a handful having carpentry or building skills, a brace each of tailors, weavers and butchers, five shoemakers and a single skilled fisherman. One man, other than Phillip and his old farm servant Henry Dodd, appears to have had significant experience of farming. Of two gardeners one was a free man sent by Joseph Banks to collect plants who decided to stay at the Cape. Of the rest with any trade at all, most were labourers or menials. Many of the women, if not already *de facto* prostitutes, soon became little better, for rum and other favours from male prisoners, guards and seamen alike.

Ill-clothed, malnourished, lousy, some infirm and sickly, disorientated and banished from all they knew by a brutal law, such was the detritus that wallowed vomiting south-west in Phillip's convoy, in most cases for ever. The Marine guards also sailed anticipating an absence of years, some taking wives and children with them. Others could not: 'Oh my God all my hopes are over of seeing my beloved wife and son', wrote the recently married Ralph Clark, their second lieutenant, when the fleet did not put into Plymouth.

Fortunately the voyage was relatively uneventful, especially in the warmer first stages, apart from some rationing of food and water. A few convict plots were easily countered, with putting in irons and flogging (neither unusual in the Navy) for troublemakers, including several incorrigible women. Later dissensions were heralded in the often harsher discipline of the Marines, one of whom got 200 lashes for passing forged coin at Rio de Janiero. Astonishingly, given the conditions, the forgeries were made by convicts on board, who were less severely punished.

Fair weather also allowed a regime of regular deck exercise while Phillip ensured the ships were kept as clean and ventilated as possible. All ports of call were foreseen in the sailing orders, Rio de Janeiro becoming necessary after adequate supplies, especially fruit, could not be found at Tenerife, and because Phillip's experience anticipated hard bargaining at Cape Town. At Rio, from 5 August to 3 September, his local reputation helped him to take on (apart from musket balls) useful plants, seeds and other supplies, and a large stock of oranges for both convicts and crews. This suggests that his views on their efficacy against scurvy were more advanced than Cook's, whose success owed more to his advocacy of 'greens' and hygiene than his mistaken trust in malt extract. In fact, the health record of the voyage was unprecedented for its nature and a tribute to Phillip's regime. It covered a total of just over 15,000 miles in 252 days, of which 184 were at sea – making the average speed an unexceptional three knots. Between

'Entrance of Rio de Janeiro (Brasil). From the Anchorage without the Sugar Loaf bearing N.W. ½ N. off Shore 2 miles', by George Raper, 1790. The 'First Fleet' at anchor, with *Sirius* in the centre and the two-masted *Supply* third to her right.

Portsmouth and Rio only sixteen people died (ten in the mephitic *Alexander*), most being those already sick on departure. By Botany Bay it had risen to forty-eight: four female convicts, thirty-six male, five convicts' children, plus a Marine, a Marine's wife and a Marine's child. This was under three per cent of a total company of about 1350, while only about a third of deaths were from scurvy. By contrast, when the Second Fleet arrived in 1790 it had already lost 267 out of 1017 convicts and was riddled with other infirmities: in 1791 the Third Fleet lost 182 out of 1864. Albeit both were run by appalling contractors, mainly experienced in the slave trade, such casualties were more typical of long and crowded voyages.

On 13 October 1787 the First Fleet anchored in Table Bay. Phillip then increased the human crowding to embark an official stock, mostly for breeding, of 'one stallion, three mares, three colts, six cows, two bulls, 44 sheep, four goats and 28 hogs' plus poultry, and all the feed for these creatures and others purchased privately by officers. He also obtained 'a vast number' of seeds and plants including citrus and other fruit trees, the Cape having a well-stocked botanical and agricultural garden. This time the Dutch proved more courteous but their merchants racked up prices, as expected. Phillip was none the less able to ensure that the convicts and his men were equally well fed on fresh provisions before the last leg of the voyage. Everyone was aware that their departure on 12 November cut them off indefinitely from 'every scene of civilization and humanized manners', in a phrase of Marine Lieutenant Tench.

On 25 November, in the southern Indian Ocean, Phillip split the fleet and went ahead in the *Supply* with the three fastest sailers (*Alexander*, *Scarborough* and *Friendship*), the others following as closely as possible. His aim was to find a settlement site and, aided by some 'convict artificers' moved into these ships, build a storehouse to speed the unloading and homeward passage of the transports. But in the stormy 'roaring forties'

'A View of Botany Bay'. While not drawn by an eyewitness, this represents the *Sirius* (flying Phillip's commodore's pendant) arriving in Botany Bay in 1788 to join the *Supply*, on the right. The rest of the First Fleet comes in from the sea beyond. Engraved by Thomas Medland after Robert Cleveley, 1789.

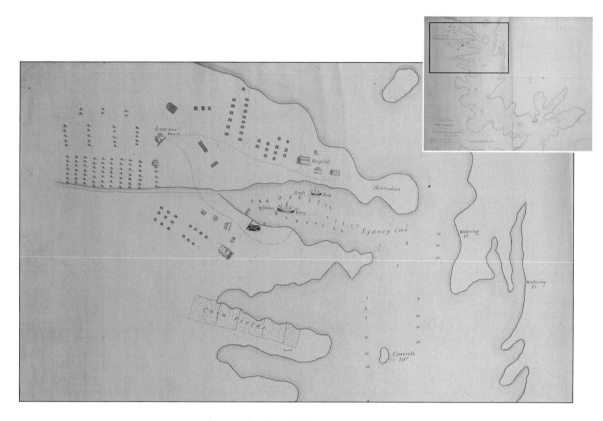

'New South Wales. Port Jackson from the Entrance up to Sydney Cove taken in Octr 1788.' The sketch plan of the early settlement round Sydney Cove has been enlarged here from the top left corner of the double-page chart of the whole harbour (inset), which also shows the depth soundings. By an unidentified amateur artist among the colonists known only as the 'Port Jackson Painter'.

weather took a hand, blowing all ships on with hatches battened down, water rationed again, galley stoves often out and growing mortality among both personnel and livestock in cold, wet conditions. The small *Supply* struggled in the vast eastward-rolling seas but the transports, including the slower convoy under John Hunter in *Sirius*, made better speed. On 3 January 1788 Phillip sighted southern Van Diemen's Land (Tasmania) and, after struggling with contrary winds, *Supply* entered Botany Bay on the 18th. Her division came in a day behind and the rest on the 20th. Taken overall, it was a remarkable achievement that a fleet of eleven should finish the passage of eighty-eight days from the Cape practically together and without major incident. However, the advance party had no time to do more than defuse an unfriendly welcome from the 'Indians', cut urgently needed grass for the livestock and catch fresh fish.

Phillip also quickly saw that the shallow bay was a poor harbour, with inadequate soil for crops and little fresh water. Without disembarking the convicts he ordered Major Ross, the Marine commandant and the colony's lieutenant-governor, to begin clearing the best available site as a precaution but on the 21st himself led a party ten miles north in three ship's boats. His destination was the inlet called Port Jackson, in which David Collins, the new colony's judge advocate, recalled that 'Captain Cook, as he passed by, thought might be found shelter for a boat'. The entrance was through two prominent outer heads that concealed a vast, deep-water, southern arm with many inlets and islands, the last of a 'Novel & Romantic appearance', according to Surgeon Arthur Smyth. Phillip explored it for two days, reporting almost prophetically to Lord Sydney that it was 'the finest harbour in the world, in which a thousand sail of the line may ride in the most perfect security'.

> [T]he different coves were examined with all possible expedition. I fixed on the one that had the best spring of water, and in which the ships can anchor so close to the shore that at very small expense quays may be made at which the largest ships may unload. This cove, which I honoured with the name of Sydney, is about a quarter of a mile across the entrance and half a mile in length.

Phillip returned to Botany Bay – today surrounded by the southern districts of modern Sydney – on 24 January 1788, but not for long. In his absence two distant ships were seen heading in, and soon confirmed suspicions that they were the *Boussole* and *Astrolabe* of Lapérouse's Pacific expedition. Governor Phillip – as he now was – would not risk being forestalled in Port Jackson and headed back immediately in *Supply*. Hunter was left to greet the French hurriedly on the 26th with an offer to send home despatches: the convoy then weighed and struggled out of the bay in contrary winds and a flurry of minor collision damage. Collins reported that Lapérouse had used Cook's chart to guide him in and was a warm admirer of their English forerunner. Surprised not to find a settlement already established, Lapérouse stayed in the bay and in contact with Phillip's party for six weeks, turning back several convict escapees who tried to join him before disappearing northward to his grim fate.

Governor Phillip

Phillip took formal possession of Sydney Cove on the morning of 26 January, Hunter arriving that evening. The male convicts were disembarked on the 27th to clear ground and put up tents for the first night ashore. Phillip rapidly decided to establish his headquarters and the female convicts on the eastern side of the cove, and the male quarters on the western side with the Marine guards and the hospital. For himself he had brought a temporary framed canvas house from England and had picked up considerable private livestock including a horse, dogs, two dozen sheep, poultry and rabbits (later a bane). His own and other gardens were quickly planted on both sides of the cove, and, on 1 February, Farm Cove to the south began earning its name with a larger area being cleared for vegetables by Dodd. On the 6th the women were landed, with predictable results: a night of debauchery and drunken riot in the scrub by convicts, seamen and Marines indiscriminately, accompanied rather than discouraged by an apocalyptic storm and lashing rain.

Order was established at a parade the next morning, with the Marines marching in to stand over the circled, squatting convicts, their band, colours, volleys of musketry and 'God Save The King' adding pageantry to the formalities. Phillip heard Collins read out his commission as governor and the letters-patent establishing the legal basis of the colony. He then gave a 'short speech, extremely well adapted to the people he had to govern' but also 'mild and humane' – at least in parts. He attempted to give hope to all who had so far behaved well and who realized that this was a new start in which only 'repetition of former demerits' would count against them. Those who did not work would not eat, since '*good* Men . . . should not be slaves for the *Bad*'. Those who helped to create a civil, ordered society would be rewarded but any 'Men & Women . . . so thoroughly abandoned in their Wickedness as to have lost every good Principle' would 'inevitably meet with the punishment which they deserved', however much it would 'distress his feelings'. He would encourage regular convict marriages but male prisoners trying to get into the women's tents at night would risk being shot: those convicted of pillaging the colony's precious breeding animals, or stealing other produce, would be hanged (the first example made being of seventeen-year-old Thomas Barrett). He hoped that they would be helped by the absence of other temptations – as escapees to the bush would soon discover, fatally – and ended by wishing them all 'reformation, happiness and prosperity, in this new country' and granting the rest of the day as a holiday.

For the next four years Phillip's steady resolution in keeping to this agenda was the bedrock of the colony's precarious existence. The beauty of Port Jackson, on which many of the First Fleet's journalists remarked, hid many thorns. The ground at Sydney Cove was rocky and took extensive labour to clear of embedded eucalyptus trees, whose timber proved practically useless except for burning. Until better wood was found, reed-thatched huts and barracks made of cabbage-palm trunks daubed with mud were miserably leaky and a haven for vermin. Phillip's convicts included only one brickmaker and, when he isolated suitable clay, it was a major achievement to build a secure storehouse with a tiled roof, a hospital building and soon also to get officers' cottages and a permanent, brick-built Government House under way – for long the only one in the colony with glass windows.

'A view of Sydney Cove, Port Jackson, March 7th 1792.' One of an important group of drawings by the Port Jackson Painter.

Food remained the critical problem in the early 'starvation years'. Animals failed to thrive and fell prey to natural and careless accident: dingoes, over-consumption of personal stock by officers and surreptitious pillage by Aborigines and convicts. Breeding rates were also inadequate until new imports came in from 1790 on. Supplementary hunting and fishing had some success but proved too erratic to rely on. Agricultural expertise was seriously lacking. First plantings inevitably put in at the wrong season either died or were sickly, some seed was weevil-infested, mice proved a problem and, later, drought as well.

Many of the convicts also unsurprisingly proved idle or simply unreformable. They stole private property, produce cultivated by the more diligent, game and fish, food from the government stores and the precious European livestock. Phillip's court backed up his promise of flogging and hanging where necessary but he also took more constructive measures to promote self-reliance. He devised a system in which reliable individuals and cohesive groups – including the free crews of *Sirius* and *Supply* – were made responsible for supporting themselves on allocated plots, or for doing other tasks whose completion left them with time to cultivate for themselves. Similarly, a dozen trustworthy convicts were formed into an effective though hated night watch to counter theft from gardens and huts after dark. The success of some of the early convict marriages also encouraged family responsibility – and families. For despite often painful rationing no one died of hunger, while the fine climate and good medical care soon raised general health and the infant-survival rate above contemporary English norms. By these means, albeit slowly, the power of example and achievable ambitions started to have a noticeably reforming effect.

Self-sustaining agriculture really began when Phillip established a farm away from Sydney Cove, on more extensive fertile ground at Parramatta – at the head of Port Jackson – in November 1788. The first year's grain harvest was kept entirely for seed but some became consumable thereafter. 1792 saw the first bumper crop and Parramatta already well established with its own Government House, storehouse and settlement. It was also there that James Ruse – a convict Cornish farmer – began the first successful personal farm, a project Phillip backed partly as an experiment in what a determined man could do. Ruse started with two government acres in November 1789 and in February 1792 Phillip made over this 'Experiment Farm' to him as the first private land grant in Australia. It had then been expanded to thirty acres supporting Ruse, his new convict wife Elizabeth – whose sentence Phillip remitted absolutely in July 1792 – their daughter and two convict labourers. It later rose to 200 acres, though Ruse eventually lost it and ended his life working for another farmer.

While Phillip insisted on good treatment of the local Eora Aborigines, the convicts' general attitude to them was poor. They quickly stole essential native weapons as 'curiosities' for trade with departing sailors, and began other maltreatment for which the Aborigines soon exacted lethal repayment to (sometimes innocent) hunters and others in the bush.

'The Governor making his best way to the Boat after being wounded by a spear sticking in his Shoulder', (detail). The Port Jackson Painter's record of Phillip's wounding on 7 September 1790 while trying to re-establish contact with the Aborigines.

Phillip refused to countenance revenge and punished those who attempted it, his best intentions inevitably fuelling the vicious cycle. His own early relations with the Aborigines were also fraught and variable, and included the desperate expedient of forcibly detaining three of them long enough to learn their language. The first, Arabanoo, detained in December 1788, ultimately stayed of his own accord but died in May 1789 in a smallpox outbreak, one of several European diseases which soon caused many native deaths. Colbee and Bennelong, captured in November 1789, had both escaped six months later. Phillip was himself nearly killed by a spear in the shoulder when leading a party to try and renew contact with them in September 1790, but he again forbade reprisals. Shortly afterwards the Aborigines sought to 'mend fences' and relationships slowly if erratically improved. In the end Phillip's diplomacy, his willingness to help the Aborigines with food and medical aid, and to welcome them into both the European community and as guests in his own house, began to normalize their presence in Sydney Cove. Where his enlightened attitude came from other than from Cook's example – itself based on wise advice in London – is hard to say, or what might have happened thereafter had it continued. Regrettably, more familiar attitudes reasserted themselves under his successors, with dire results for Aboriginal society. It was to Phillip's credit that, when he left Australia, Bennelong was one of two Aborigines who accompanied him and lived to return home in 1795, though the other, Yemmerrawannie, died in England in 1794.

With nature, inexperience and human folly against him, the new Governor had to issue more of the imported dry stores (such as flour) than expected and then steadily reduce rations as stocks became critically low. The convicts' general good health on the voyage dipped seriously after arrival, affecting their ability to work. Drink and the dislocations of exile also took their toll, with runaways dying or being killed in the bush. Others succumbed to depression, madness in one or two cases and general quarrels. In October 1788, with no news of when further supplies would arrive from

England – or further convict mouths to feed – John Hunter left for Cape Town in *Sirius* for essential replenishments. He took the longer but easier option of sailing round the world via Cape Horn, before returning in May 1789 with 120,000 pounds of flour (four months' supply), new seed stock and much-needed medical supplies. He also brought the first letters from home, which improved morale without giving any news of relief.

A major cause for resentment among Phillip's men – primarily the Marine officers and troops – was his policy of issuing equal rations to all and housing both convicts and non-convicts the same way. As with his attitude to the Aborigines, this egalitarianism ran against hierarchical norms. It was impossible to argue with, however, since he applied the same rationing rules to himself and in mid-1790 put all his considerable private supplies into the common stock. There were further particular problems with the Marines. Their officers resented the extension of their role as guards into being working overseers, the men that their own disciplinary code was often harsher than the convicts', and that Phillip also applied justice impartially, hanging six Marines at once for systematic theft from government stores in 1789.

The problem began at the top with the Marine commandant Robert Ross, described by a subordinate as 'without exception the most disagreeable commanding officer I ever knew'. He felt himself slighted by a lack of consultation, although Phillip's commission allowed him to govern without a formal council, and naval captains were neither required nor expected to consult more than they thought fit. Phillip clearly explained his own orders to Ross, and London's expectations, but he continued to be a self-sufficient master of detail in managing the colony and Ross a touchy bad example of subordinate leadership.

Such 'want of temper' in Ross and other officers added to more material problems until March 1790, when Phillip dispatched him in *Sirius* and *Supply* with 280 convict men, women and children to Norfolk Island, 1000 miles off the coast to the north-west. He had already sent a party of twenty-two there in February 1789 under King, again to head off possible French occupation. King reported that the soil was rich and cultivable. A further forty went in October, then Ross's party and many others after the arrival of the Second and Third Fleets. All were sustained by a brutal and eventually exterminating dependence on the mutton bird, a migratory species that spent March to August on the island and made excellent eating. Despite many difficulties, the establishment of a successful sub-colony seemed possible but ultimately circumstances were against this. The timber from the tall island pines proved to be too brittle for masts and the local flax too coarse and difficult to work for canvas by normal methods. More

'His Majesty's Ship *Sirius* in Sydney Cove 1789' (right) and 'His Majesty's Brig *Supply* 1790 … ', both by George Raper. *Supply* (left) is shown off Lord Howe Island, which she discovered on her first voyage to Norfolk Island, landing there on the way back.

Edward Riou (1762–1801). Riou was a lieutenant when he commanded the *Guardian*. This miniature by Samuel Shelley shows him as a captain, just before he was killed fighting at the Battle of at Copenhagen while serving under Nelson.

critically, while free agriculture could have supported the island under good government, the sadistic incompetence of its regime after 1800, under the New South Wales Corps, turned it into a living hell for new convicts and those already emancipated there, and it was abandoned in 1813–14.

By early 1790, poor crop yields and diminished stores meant that starvation loomed at Port Jackson, a principal reason for the departure of Ross's party. No one then knew that Phillip's first reports home had resulted in the storeship *Guardian* sailing from England the previous September. Commanded by Lieutenant Edward Riou – a former midshipman with Cook – she carried two years' stores, agricultural supervisors and two dozen convicts chosen for their farming or building skills. She also collected many more plants and animals from the Cape but then hit an iceberg in the Indian Ocean in December 1789 and lost her rudder. Riou's brilliant seamanship got her back to Cape Town, where she was wrecked in a storm. Had Riou arrived, *Sirius* would probably not have sailed with Ross to Norfolk Island, from where *Supply* returned on 5 April 1790 bringing the dreadful news that she too had been wrecked on the surrounding reef, though without casualties.

On 3 June 1790, hungry despondency after loss of the *Sirius* was relieved when Phillip's lookout station on South Head signalled the arrival of the *Lady Juliana*. Nearly eleven months out from Plymouth, she brought 225 female convicts but, more importantly, transformed the morale of the colonists. They now learnt of the loss of the *Guardian*, of the outbreak of the French Revolution, and that *Lady Juliana* was the first of a 'Second Fleet' which had all arrived by the end of the month – the storeship *Gorgon*, and the transports *Neptune*, *Surprize* and *Scarborough* (again).

The extra mouths to feed, the hundreds who landed sick, the fact that many of the newcomers were too old or infirm to work and the disruptions created by the injection of a fresh criminal element added to immediate problems which, from July 1790 to October 1791, included

'Distressing Situation of the *Guardian* Sloop, Capt. Riou, after striking on a floating Island of Ice.' The ship's rudder and part of her keel were torn off but Riou got her back to Cape Town. Much of her cargo went on later to Port Jackson. Aquatint published by Thomas Tegg, 1809.

drought. None the less, the Second Fleet's arrival proved a watershed. With it came further stores, plants, animals and some of the more skilled convicts and supervisors originally sent in the *Guardian*, all of which helped to strengthen the colony and give Phillip means to help those, like Ruse, who were trying make their own way. He also sent *Supply* to obtain further supplies from Batavia (Jakarta). She returned in October 1790 followed in December by a hired storeship, these cargoes helping carry them through 1791. The sickly Third Fleet straggled in between August and October of that year, when Phillip sent the *Atlantic* back to Calcutta for further supplies just as the drought broke and ensured the good harvest of 1792. *Atlantic* returned in June, two more storeships came in from England by that November and thereafter Sydney's transformation from harbour to regular port began (see illustration on p. 90). By the end of 1792 there were more than 4000 colonists under Phillip's jurisdiction, some 1100 of these being on Norfolk Island. By then the principal mainland agriculture comprised 1000 productive government acres and more than 500 in private hands, most on the better land round Parramatta. Phillip had also made land grants to sixty-six people there or nearby by that October. Fifty-three of these were emancipated convicts, though one of Phillip's causes for regret was that many of the abler men preferred to work their way home when their sentences expired.

The other great change was the arrival with the Second Fleet of the first companies of the New South Wales Corps, under Major Francis Grose, to relieve Ross's Marines. Grose had been wounded fighting in America but revived his career by helping to raise the Corps specifically for Australian service. Unlike the Marines they were intended to settle, many bringing wives. The calibre of the Corps' men was poor but its role included the civilian administrative and supervisory tasks to which Ross's officers had objected. Phillip himself foresaw that substantial expansion of agriculture would require a quasi-military organization but was much disturbed in later years by the immediate direction this took.

Grose was encouraged by what he saw on arrival. As the new lieutenant-governor he inherited Ross's farm and after Phillip left he and a short-term successor commanded the colony until 1795, when Hunter returned as governor. Grose militarized the administration, replaced civilian magistrates with his own officers, abolished Phillip's egalitarian methods and accelerated land grants to his own men – most significantly offering his officers 100 acres each with ten convict labourers to work it at government expense. The control of labour was largely vested in his new regimental paymaster, Lieutenant John Macarthur – a central figure in the military 'mafia' which quickly established itself as Australia's first governing and property-owning élite. This shift was commercially launched in 1793 when Macarthur organized the cartel that, using access to credit against pay, bought 7500 gallons of rum and the other cargo of an American trader, and sold it on in the colony at a huge profit. The transaction prefigured the Corps' ongoing control of trade through

'Sydney Bay, Norfolk Island, to which place a portion of the Pitcairn Islanders are in Course of Removal, May 1855.' Forty years after Governor Phillip's early Norfolk Island colony was abandoned, missionary activity and administrative policy led to some of the descendants of the *Bounty* mutineers being resettled there. Based on a drawing by J.Glen Wilson of HMS *Herald*.

Bronze bust (1932) 'in honour of Admiral Arthur Phillip, Citizen of London, founder and first Governor of Australia' in the church of St Mary-le-Bow, Cheapside, London. The bust is by Charles Leonard Hartwell RA (1873–1951). It is based on a portrait of 1786 by Francis Wheatley, now in Australia, and was originally in St Mildred's, Bread Street, which was destroyed by bombing in 1941.

Sydney, aided by emancipated convict trader allies, their gains being used to buy up land from the many less successful ex-convict farmers. By these means arriving transportees effectively became slaves to the private benefit of the 'Rum Corps', as it became known, and remained in its thrall after sentences expired.

Last campaigns

Phillip was not there to see it. Tired and ill by the autumn of 1792, he anticipated formal permission to return home, embarking in the *Atlantic* on 11 December with 'the honors due to his rank and situation in the colony'. With him went his two Aboriginal protégés, live kangaroos, dingoes and other animals, and natural specimens to add to those he had already sent back to Banks and others. He reached England in May 1793 via the Cape and Rio. After reporting in London and clarifying legal matters arising from the death (in 1792) of his estranged wife, he resigned his governorship in October and went to Bath to recover his health, though requesting further active service. There he met forty-three-year-old Isabella Whitehead, a well-provided spinster, and they embarked on what seems to have been a late but happy marriage in May 1794.

Well regarded in naval, government and scientific circles, Phillip continued to advise on Australia and to support the careers of valued former subordinates there, particularly Phillip Gidley King, who succeeded Hunter as governor in 1800. He himself returned to active service in 1796, commanding in rapid succession the *Alexander* (in which he had been a lieutenant), *Swiftsure* and *Blenheim*. In the last two he was in the Earl of St Vincent's Mediterranean Fleet, gaining both his and Nelson's approval, and pleased St Vincent further in conducting a delicate diplomatic mission at Lisbon for three months in 1797–98. It was thus the worst disappointment of his life when the Earl allowed him to be replaced as captain of the *Blenheim*, after Rear-Admiral Frederick took her as his flagship in February 1798. Worse, in retrospect, was the fact that Phillip only left the *Swiftsure* at St Vincent's request, which denied him captain's glory in her at the Battle of the Nile that August. It was also characteristic of the time that, despite his generous pay and pension as founding governor of New South Wales, it gained him none of the public honours granted to captains for such fighting service, often very brief.

Phillip never had another ship and his last naval roles were in command of the Sea Fencibles – volunteer coastal defence forces – in Hampshire, and as general inspector of both the Impress Service (from 1801), and the Sea Fencibles (1803–05). In December 1806 he and his wife moved permanently to Bath, where early in 1808 he had a stroke that left him partly paralysed in his right side, although clear in mind and able to resume a quiet social life. He reached the rank of full admiral by seniority in May 1814 and died with the fading summer on 31 August that year, aged seventy-five.

CHAPTER THREE

'THE SPIRIT OF DISCOVERY': THE TRAGIC VOYAGE OF LAPÉROUSE

*'The former spirit of discovery seemed to
have vanished entirely' – Lapérouse*

On 26 January 1788, two French ships, *Astrolabe* and *Boussole*, sailed into Botany Bay. They were nearing the end of an ambitious voyage of scientific exploration in the Pacific Ocean, begun nearly three years earlier, in 1785, under the command of Jean-François de Galaup, Comte de La Pérouse. His ships had originally been under orders to visit New Zealand rather than Australia, but new instructions from Paris had reached him in Kamchatka, on the Russian Pacific coast, that he was to investigate reports that Britain was planning to establish a new settlement in New South Wales. He arrived less than a week after the First Fleet, just as they were on the point of moving up the coast to the more suitable site of Port Jackson.

The two strange ships caused a certain amount of conjecture, if not consternation, in Botany Bay: were they Dutch and coming to dispossess the British? Could they be British ships with stores? If they were French, were the two countries at war again? In fact they were still at peace and the French were welcomed warmly when it was learnt that this was the famous Lapérouse expedition. The benefits of science were considered universal at the time and the great series of eighteenth-century European voyages of exploration, motivated, it was believed, by 'the enlarged and benevolent design of promoting the happiness of the human species', were seen as epitomizing these lofty ideals. In consequence, it was not unusual for scientific ships of enemy nations to be helped, even during time of war. 'Europeans are all compatriots at this distance from their countries', commented Lapérouse on their welcome from the British, although in practice he found that their 'offers of assistance were restricted to good wishes for the ultimate success of our voyage' rather than the stores the French desperately needed. In fairness to Governor Phillip, the young

'John Francis Galaup de la Pérouse, Commodore in the French Navy, born at Alby in 1741'. Engraving by James Heath, 1798. 'Lapérouse' is the usual modern French spelling.

JOHN FRANCIS GALAUP
DE LA PÉROUSE,
Commodore in the French Navy, born at Alby in 1741.

colony had little enough for itself.

The many savants on board the two French ships made the most of their time in what had become, since Cook's visit nearly twenty years earlier, natural history's most famous bay. The French botanists collected specimens and also planted some of the seeds that they had brought with them, adding to the varieties that Phillip's ships had carried out from Britain. The astronomers set up their instruments ashore in a temporary camp and made their observations. Lapérouse himself sent back copies of his journal and charts to the Ministry of Marine with the returning British convict transports. The French and British officers socialized happily, while on a more sombre note the French chaplain, Father Receveur, who had died as a result of wounds received during an attack on the ships' boats in Samoa, became, as far as is known, the first Frenchman to be buried in Australia. After a month *Astrolabe* and *Boussole* left Botany Bay planning, as Lapérouse informed both his minister and Governor Phillip, a sweep north and east into the Pacific before turning west for Ile de France (Mauritius) in the Indian Ocean and then home to Brest. They never reached their destination and it would be nearly forty years before the mystery of their disappearance was solved.

It had been the largest and best-equipped voyage of scientific exploration ever mounted by France to that date. Since Louis-Antoine de Bougainville had crossed the Pacific and landed in Tahiti just before Cook

Louis XVI of France giving instructions to Jean-François de Galaup, Comte de La Pérouse, 29 June 1785. Oil painting by Nicolas-André Monsiaux, 1817.

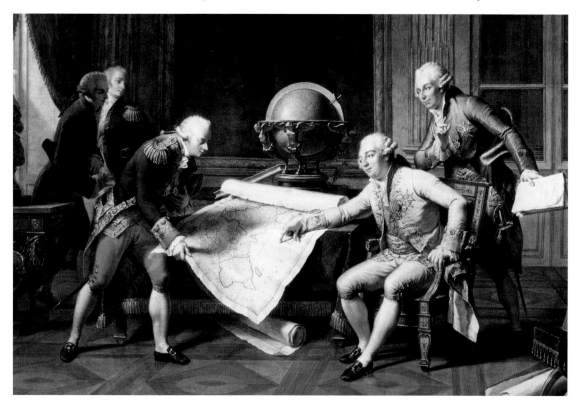

'Tableau des Decouvertes du Capne. Cook, & de la Pérouse', hand-coloured etching by Jacques Grasset St-Sauveur, 1797. In 1804 Josef Dufour based a series of wallpapers on the etching, claiming in the prospectus that 'the reader of histories of travel can imagine himself among those nations … and become familiar with their costumes and the diversity of nature.'

The caption below the image lists: '1. *Hab*[itant]s *de Nootka* [Nootka Sound, Vancouver Island]. – 2. … *de la Zélande* [New Zealand]. – 3. … *de l'Entrée de Prince Guillaume* [Prince William Sound, Alaska]. – 4. … *de l'Ile de Pâques* [Easter Island]. – 5. … *de la Baye du Norton* [Norton Bay, Alaska]. – 6. … *des Iles Sandwich* [Hawaiian Islands]. – 7. … *de Tanna* [Tanna, Vanuatu]. – 8. … *de Ste Christine* [Tahuata, Marquesas Islands]. – 9. … *de la Baye de Castries* [De-Kastri Bay, Republic of Tartary]. – 10. … *de la Baye ou Port des Français* [Lituya Bay, Alaska] – 11. … *Maouna* [Upolu, Samoa]. – 12. … *Macao* [Macao, China]. – 13. … *de la Baye de Langle* [probably Tomari, Sakhalin]. – 14. … *de la Conception* [Concepción, Chile]. – 15. … *de la Baye de Manilles* [Manila, Philippines]. – 16. … *des Iles Pelew* [Palau Islands]. – 17. … *Oonolaska* [Aleutian Islands]. – 18. … *Ulieta* [Raiatea, Society Islands]. – 19. … *des Iles des Marquises* [Marquesas Islands]. – 20. … *de l'Ile des Amis* [Tonga]. – 21. … *de la Nouvelle Caledonie* [New Caledonia]. – 22. … *d'Otaïti* [Tahiti, Society Islands]. – 23. … *d'Anaamoku* [Nomuka, Tonga]. – 24. … *de Hapaée* [Ha'apai, Tonga]'

in 1768, France had launched four voyages to the South Seas, but none had been particularly distinguished and one had ended tragically. National pride, if nothing else, insisted that Lapérouse's voyage should be of a scale to rival, if not exceed, those of the famous Captain Cook. But there was a problem with this almost immediately as any new voyage to the Pacific in the wake of Cook could do little more than fill in the few gaps left by the great navigator. The director of the Dépôt des Cartes et Plans, Claret de Fleurieu, had argued in the original proposal that while Cook had made Europe 'aware of the existence of vast countries, scattered islands and clusters of islands' in the Pacific, 'it must not be thought that we have a complete knowledge of the Earth; and in particular, of the North-West coasts of America, of those of Asia which face them, and of the islands that must be scattered in the sea that separates the parts of these two continents'. Orders were accordingly drawn up which directed Lapérouse to concentrate on the less-well-covered areas of the north and west Pacific. What the expedition would inevitably lack in major new discoveries would be more than compensated for by detailed surveys of those areas only touched on by Cook, and the range and depth of the scientific research. Louis XVI, himself a keen geographer, took a close personal interest in the voyage, helping to plan its route and discussing its objectives with Lapérouse, while the names of the ships, *Astrolabe* and *Boussole* ('astrolabe' and 'compass'), underlined its navigational aims. This was exploration as high-profile national enterprise. Although France and Britain were at peace, and their scientific communities cooperated informally on the preparations for the voyage, scientific exploration was by now inescapably part of national rivalry and was effectively being used by France as a way of continuing war by other, more peaceable, means.

Lapérouse was born in 1741 in Albi in south-west France. Although his family had been climbing the social ladder for generations, it was still very much *petit noblesse* and the name 'de La Pérouse' was only acquired for him when he decided to join the navy, which was a far more class-structured institution than its British counterpart. He was an experienced seaman and navigator who had made his name during the American War of Independence. Significantly, in the context of his Pacific voyage, he had gained a reputation as a humanitarian commander when, during an attack on British trading posts in Hudson's Bay in 1782, he had treated his prisoners courteously and left provisions at the destroyed base for those who were away hunting at the time and who would otherwise have been unable to survive the winter. His second-in-command and the captain of *Astrolabe* was Fleuriot de Langle, an equally experienced officer who had sailed with Lapérouse on the Hudson's Bay raid.

Lapérouse was to take no fewer than fifteen civilian scientists including artists, astronomers, civil engineers, surveyors, botanists, an ornithologist and a clockmaker; even the expedition's chaplain, the unfortunate Father Receveur, was an accomplished botanist. In this the voyage departed from the principle that had eventually been adopted in Britain. After Cook's difficulties with Banks over the structural changes needed to accommodate the large scientific party on the *Resolution*, and his even more uneasy relationship with the naturalist Johann Reinhold Forster on the voyage itself, the number of civilian scientists on the third voyage was cut dramatically. Cook only took an artist and an astronomer, and the rest of the scientific work was carried out by the officers, a practice from which the Admiralty would henceforth only rarely depart. In France in 1785, however, there was real excitement within the scientific community as its members competed for places on this prestigious expedition: the young

Napoléon Bonaparte, who was shining in the mathematics class at the École Militaire, applied unsuccessfully, while Georg Forster, the scientist who had accompanied his father and Cook on the second voyage, was briefly considered but eventually not invited, as it was thought that it would ultimately be 'more interesting to perhaps consider the same things in a different way'.

The head botanist was to be Joseph de la Martinière. France had long been aware of the commercial possibilities of plants from overseas and since the 1750s colonial administrators in the French West Indies had been required to send samples of plants back to the Musée d'Histoire Naturelle in Paris. Georges de Buffon, the eminent but now ageing author of the influential *Histoire Naturelle* and head of the museum, was consulted on the question of appointing a suitable gardener to look after the plants on the voyage, and he referred the matter to Thouin, the King's head gardener, who in turn suggested a young man called Jean-Nicolas Collignon and drew up a detailed list of instructions for him on how to collect plants and seeds and store them at sea. While at Brest preparing for the voyage, Collignon fell out with la Martinière, who believed that a botanical scientist should be in charge of a mere gardener, whereas Collignon thought he should be answerable only to Lapérouse. Although Lapérouse appeared to side with Collignon, and tried to keep the two men apart by transferring la Martinière to *Boussole*, the argument was merely a foretaste of the squabbles that would break out periodically during the voyage.

The botanical objectives were twofold. The King's instructions to Lapérouse specified that on the one hand the botanists were to collect plants and specimens which 'would enrich Europe', and on the other they were to introduce useful European species to 'newly discovered countries', for:

> Of all the benefits which the King's generosity can bestow on the inhabitants of newly discovered countries, plants that can help feed mankind are without doubt those which will bring them the most lasting benefits, and can best increase their happiness.

A glazed cabinet for transporting plants made for the Lapérouse expedition. From the notebook of Gaspard Duché de Vancy.

To this end Collignon carried fifty-nine live fruit trees and shrubs and enormous quantities of vegetable seeds and bulbs. When collecting rather than planting he was also instructed to ignore as much as possible the distractions of beautiful and exotic flora and concentrate instead on useful plants. Special cases were designed and built and sent to Brest already carefully packed with the live plants, for Thouin considered that they were as vulnerable on the two-week journey from Paris as they would be on the voyage to the Pacific. The plant boxes were an advanced design with three layers of protection. The first was a mesh of fine tin wire that protected the plants from normal shipboard accidents. On top of that was a close-fitting panel of glass designed to be in place virtually all the time. Watering was carried out through two holes in the sides, which would remain open except in the most extreme weather conditions to allow the air to circulate freely in the box. The third level of protection was hinged wooden shuttering, which sealed the box from the elements and prevented undue loss of moisture. Thouin thought that the plants should be able to last two weeks without watering. Forty years later Nathaniel Ward developed the Wardian Case in Britain following a similar principle, and this was to revolutionize the notoriously difficult business of transporting plants by sea.

Astrolabe and *Boussole* sailed from Brest in August 1785, heading for Cape Horn and into the Pacific Ocean, which they were to cross before beginning their investigations in the west Pacific. Lapérouse was given considerable freedom to deviate from his orders as circumstances dictated and he took advantage of this immediately. Their first port of call in the Pacific was in Chile, at Concepción, where they stayed for three weeks before setting off for Easter Island, the most easterly of the Polynesian islands. The visit was as brief as it had been for Cook's *Resolution*, the two ships staying for less than twenty-four hours. Easter Island was bleak and its lack of vegetation created a starkly different landscape from the luxuriant greenery found on the many other Polynesian islands. In 1774, Georg and J. R. Forster had described the island as an ecological disaster: 'Its wretched soil, loaded with innumerable stones, furnishes a Flora of only 20 species; among these, ten are cultivated; not one grows to a tree, and almost all are low, shrivelled and dry.'

It was obvious to the French that they had landed among a people who would benefit considerably from the introduction of European plants and vegetables. Accordingly, Collignon set about sowing cabbages, carrots, pumpkins, maize, beet and trees in places he thought them likely to succeed. Thouin's instructions were typically detailed on this and we can assume that Collignon chose his 'favourable aspects' with care and

Medal commemorating the departure of *Boussole* and *Astrolabe* from Brest in June 1785, by B. Duvivier, 1785. The ships' departure was, in fact, delayed until August.

'Islanders and ornaments of Easter Island', pen and ink sketch by Gaspard Duché de Vancy.

prepared the ground thoroughly. As they left within twenty-four hours, however, Collignon could not have spent much time establishing the plantation; neither, one imagines, would he have been able to fulfil Thouin's wish to 'inspire the love of gardening in some of the natives' which, if he could also make them understand 'the importance of the vegetables', would 'fill twice the aim of doing good that one hopes from the mission'. In fact, Lapérouse wrote in his journal, the Easter Islanders seemed singularly disinterested in the 'benefits' that Europe was bringing:

> We didn't land on their island to do them anything other
> than good: we loaded them with presents; we cultivated the
> weak with caresses, particularly the children. We sowed all
> sorts of useful grains in their fields. In their houses we left
> pigs, goats and sheep, which will in all likelihood multiply.
> Nevertheless, they threw stones at us, and they stole
> everything that they could manage to lift.

Since Bougainville's voyage had been published twenty years earlier describing Tahiti in terms of classical beauty and simplicity, Polynesians had come to embody the Rousseauesque Noble Savage living in harmony with Nature. Rousseau's conception had never gained universal acceptance; it was only one of a number of competing theories of human origins, but was far stronger in France than in Britain, especially among the classically

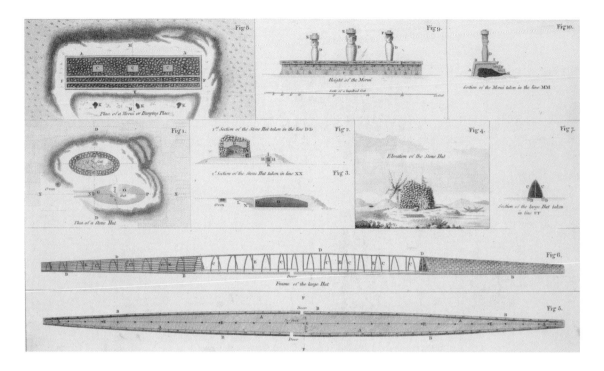

'Geometrical details of the monuments of Easter Island', from *Charts and Plates to La Pérouse's Voyage*, 1798.

educated classes from whom the scientists on board *Astrolabe* and *Boussole* were drawn. The Noble Savage was a simplified part of what was actually a far more sophisticated theory but at its heart was a belief in the essential good of humankind, in a primitive, 'untouched' state once shared by all peoples in which no one knew jealousy, greed, deceit or hate. These vices were supposed to be the by-products of an overcivilized Western society: the proper business of enlightened European travellers, therefore, was not to infect 'natural man' with the diseases of civilization, but simply to help to improve their living condition by introducing useful crafts or manufactures, for example, or those plants and vegetables cultivated in Europe. While many of the scientists on board the French ships would have seen Collignon's plantings in that philosophical light, others, including Lapérouse, did not. The belief in the Polynesian Noble Savage had already taken a severe battering after the killings of Cook in Hawaii in 1779 and the French navigator Marion du Fresne in New Zealand in 1772, after which even Rousseau professed himself shocked that the 'children of nature' could behave in such a way.

The voyage continued north to the Sandwich Islands (Hawaii) where, mindful of Cook's fate, Lapérouse was careful to protect his landing parties, and then further north to Alaska, where he gave himself three months to explore the North American coastline down to Monterey in California. The northern part of this coast had taken on a new significance to Europe after Cook's discovery of the trade in sea-otter furs, and although the aim of Lapérouse's voyage was scientific exploration, as befitted its royal backing, commercial exploitation had always lurked in the

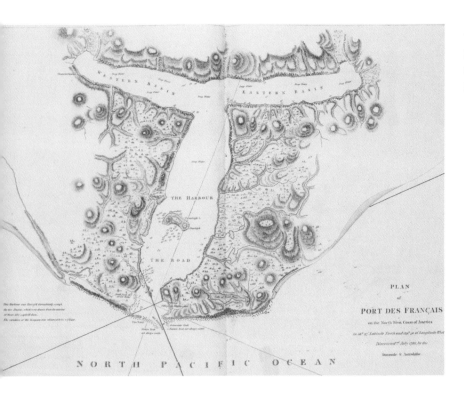

'Plan of Port des Français on the North West Coast of America', from *Charts and Plates to La Pérouse's Voyage*, 1798.

background. Lapérouse's ridiculously ambitious survey plan took no account of the intricate nature of the coast; it was to take the British navigator George Vancouver three full seasons to survey the same area. Although it did not help that Lapérouse's ships were held back by the fog, just as Cook's had been ten years earlier, the French survey actually advanced European knowledge of this coastline very little. A few places where the ships anchored for a few days, such as Port des Français about 600 miles north of Nootka Sound, were surveyed and studied to a very high standard. When the size of Port des Français became obvious to Lapérouse he hoped that he had found the entrance to the North-West Passage – 'Imagine a vast basin, whose depth in the centre is impossible to estimate, edged by great, steep, snow-covered mountains', he wrote; 'this is the channel by which we planned to enter into the heart of America' – but this hope was dashed when they followed the two arms at the head of the bay only to find that both ended almost immediately in huge glaciers.

The botanists were also disappointed. Although there was a rich supply of greenstuff, which the seamen ate in soups and salads, as well as large numbers of flowering plants and berries, Lapérouse noted that 'none of this vegetation is unknown in Europe; M. la Martinière found during his various excursions only three plants which he believes to be new, and one knows that a botanist can make a similar find in the environs of Paris'. Neither did the Tlingit people impress Lapérouse: he described them, their customs and their environment at some length but his underlying attitude is summed up in the dismissive comment that they were 'as rough and

'A Woman of Port des Français'.
Engraving by James Heath after
Gaspard Duché de Vancy, from
*Charts and Plates to La Pérouse's
Voyage*, 1798.

barbarous as their soil is stony and untilled'. European
reactions to the peoples of the north-west coast of
America were complicated and often contradictory.
Although Lapérouse, for example, condemned them
as barbarous he also saw their cultures as being more
advanced than those of the widely admired
Polynesians, who had become the standard by which
'primitives' were judged. The Tlingit could 'forge iron,
work copper, spin the hair of various animals and sew
with this wool a material similar to our tapestries'.
They were also keen and shrewd traders, Lapérouse
noticing that the population of the bay quadrupled
during his visit as a steady stream of canoes loaded
with furs arrived to take advantage of the unexpected
commercial opportunity represented by the French ships.

The harbour had been charted accurately by the surveyors de Monneron
and Bernizet, but shortly before the ships were due to leave Lapérouse
ordered three boats to complete the survey by sounding the depth of the
water around the narrow entrance, through which the tide could rush at up
to nine knots. The French ships had only entered this dangerous passage
with considerable difficulty, Lapérouse admitting that 'never in the thirty
years I have spent at sea have I seen two ships so near destruction'. He placed
the boats under the command of his first lieutenant, d'Escures, 'a Knight of
St. Louis who [had himself] commanded some of the King's ships'. Ignoring
his captain's written and verbal orders to approach the pass only at slack
water, and not to approach it at all if there was a swell, d'Escures took the
boats in while the tide was still running fast and there was a heavy sea
breaking on the reefs; two of the boats, including d'Escures's, went too close
and were sucked into the current and capsized. There were no survivors and
no bodies were ever recovered. Lapérouse erected a monument to the sailors
on Cenotaph Island and the physicist, de Lamanon, composed a short
tribute: '*A l'Entrée du Port, ont peri, vingt un braves marins, qui que vous soyés,
mêlés vos larmes aux notres*' (At the entrance to this port, twenty-one brave
sailors perished. Whoever you may be, add your tears to ours).

The ships then made their way south, sailing past what would become
Vancouver Island without discovering its insularity or spotting the
entrance to the huge sound behind it, down the Oregon and California
coasts to the new Spanish colony of Monterey. The Spaniards may have
viewed Lapérouse's arrival with as much suspicion as would the British in
Botany Bay, for the French ships were one more worrying sign that
Spain's traditional monopoly of the Pacific was under threat, but the
governor was generous in his welcome and the ships finally left after a
ten-day stay loaded down with fresh food. They headed across the Pacific
to Macao in China, which they reached on 1 January 1787, unexpectedly
discovering and nearly coming to grief on French Frigate Shoal, far to the
north-west of the Sandwich Islands.

Macao had been trading with Europe since Portugal had leased the island from China in the early sixteenth century, so the scientists sensibly decided to take advantage of the comforts of home while they were available and rented a house in the town. They omitted to inform Lapérouse, however, or even let him know where they could be found, and he got his revenge by placing them all under arrest when they finally returned to the ships. Both sides sent strongly worded complaints to Fleurieu, who decided to ignore them, presumably working on the assumption that there was nothing he could do from such a distance and that the problems would have resolved themselves anyway by the time the expedition returned to France. The ships then left Macao, taking six Chinese sailors with them to make up for the losses in Port des Français, and visited Manila in the Philippines before heading north between Korea and Japan, conscious that for the first time they were sailing into waters that few Europeans had navigated and which none had surveyed. Here Lapérouse was able to make a real contribution to cartographic knowledge. As usual, the scientists landed and took samples when they could, with Collignon planting and collecting, often in appalling conditions. At Castries Bay on the coast of Tartary he tried to light a fire with gunpowder to thaw out his freezing hands, but his thumb was broken when the powder exploded.

In August 1787 they reached Kamchatka, the most easterly point of Siberia, where Captain Clerke had been buried in 1779 towards the end of Cook's third voyage. It was here that Lapérouse received his orders to investigate Botany Bay as well as the pleasant news that he had been promoted. Before heading south he took the precaution of arranging to send home his up-to-date journal, charts and notes with Barthélémy de Lesseps, a young diplomat who had come on the voyage as Russian interpreter: it took him more than a year to get back to Paris. (De Lesseps's nephew, Ferdinand, would later build the Suez Canal.)

'Costumes des habitans de la Baye de Langle Sur Lisle de Chotka' showing the inhabitants of Castries Bay on the coast of Tartary, China, 1787. Pen and ink drawing by Gaspard Duché de Vancy.

Lapérouse sailed south in a broad arc through the Pacific Ocean, taking his ships through the Samoan islands. Here tragedy struck again. In a letter sent to Thouin from Botany Bay, Collignon described the incident:

> Since I had the honour of writing you my last letter from Kamchatka, we've disembarked in [a] few more landing places. Amongst others at an island in the Navigators [Samoa], where I was hoping to take some roots of the bread-fruit tree, of which there were many in great quantity. But on the second day of our visit, which I had planned for this task, and for which I had landed the necessary instruments, [there was] a tragic, cruel scene where we lost several men, some of the first rank of officers, and I just escaped becoming a victim myself, having been wounded in several places. But I, as well as several others, had the happiness of escaping from the hands of our assassins, inhabitants and indigenous people of these parts, who behaved in this extreme way despite the fact that our procedures were the most humanitarian imaginable. But unfortunately we have been dupes of our own good nature, and this is what has denied me any possibility up to the present of procuring this most valuable plant.

They had arrived at Tutuila on 10 December 1787 and, after what had appeared to be a friendly reception, the captain of *Astrolabe*, de Langle, told Lapérouse that he wanted to land and take on board fresh water. In this, Lapérouse acknowledged, de Langle was following 'the system used by Captain Cook [who] believed that fresh water was a hundred times better than the water we had in the hold'. But Lapérouse did not subscribe to this theory and argued in turn that the ships had enough water to get them to Botany Bay and that landing was therefore an unnecessary risk. De Langle insisted and Lapérouse finally agreed, writing later in his journal that 'M. de Langle was a man with such judgment and such qualities that these facts more than anything else caused me to give my consent ... '. It is interesting to put de Langle's refusal to accept Lapérouse's orders alongside that of d'Escures in Port des Français and to speculate whether they indicate any deeper problems on the expedition. Social rank was a perennial problem in the pre-Revolutionary French navy; incidents where subordinate officers refused to take orders from their military superiors because they were their social inferiors were neither unknown nor conducive to the efficient running of ships. D'Escures was the son of an admiral and de Langle a *vicomte*, the social superior of Lapérouse, and it was rumoured that de Langle had been considered for command of the expedition for that reason. While the two men had sailed together for a number of years and clearly liked and respected each other, social rank may have complicated their relationship. Whatever the reason, de Langle had his way at Samoa and led the boats ashore.

Several of the scientists, including Collignon and the physicist Lamanon, joined the watering party of sixty men. Because of the lie of the land, the boats were soon out of sight of the ships and when they approached the shore they discovered that the tide was out, which meant that the boats grounded, vulnerably, a considerable distance from the beach. A number of Samoans came out to the boats and began trading with the sailors and the situation appeared fairly peaceful. The seamen started to fill the barrels from the freshwater stream flowing down to the beach, while Collignon began to explore the area around the beach, putting samples of interesting plants into a sack he had slung over his back. According to Lapérouse, who tried to piece together the chain of events later on, the situation started to deteriorate rapidly when the seamen and islanders began arguing about price. By this time more than a thousand Samoans had gathered on the beach and Collignon began to move back to the boats just as the situation broke into confused and bloody conflict. Both Lamanon and de Langle were killed in the fight.

Astrolabe and *Boussole* sailed on for Botany Bay, whence they were to depart on 10 March 1788 and so disappear into the Pacific Ocean. By early 1790 concerns about the expedition's fate were being expressed publicly in France. As the years passed with still no word, the story generated its own literature with poems, plays, pantomimes and melodramas appearing in Dutch, English, French and Italian. The loss of Lapérouse touched all of Europe although, admittedly, not to the same degree as the death of Cook. In February 1791 Fleurieu declared them officially lost. Pressure grew for a search expedition and later that year the National Assembly gave Bruny D'Entrecasteaux command of two ships, *Recherche* and *Espérance* ('search' and 'hope'), which finally sailed in September 1791. It was to be both a rescue mission and a voyage of discovery, for D'Entrecasteaux took with him almost as many scientists as had Lapérouse.

But where to begin the search? Lapérouse's last letter from Botany Bay said that he was planning to strike out into the Pacific in order to complete his original instructions to explore the islands of the western Pacific. This meant that he would sail to 'the south of New Caledonia, Mendaña's Santa Cruz, the south coast of de Surville's Arsacides, and Bougainville's Louisiades, to see if they join New Guinea or not. By the end of July 1788', Lapérouse wrote:

> I will pass between New Guinea and New Holland by
> another channel than the *Endeavour*'s, if there be one. I will
> visit, during September and part of October, the Gulf of
> Carpentaria and western New Holland as far as Van
> Diemen's Land, but in a way that will enable me to sail
> north early enough to reach the Ile de France.

This was a lot of ocean to cover and D'Entrecasteaux's search was complicated by a report from Phillip's deputy, Captain Hunter of the *Sirius*, that he believed Lapérouse may have been wrecked east of Timor,

'Massacre of De Langle, Lamanon and Ten Others of the Two Crews', engraving by James Heath after Nicolas Ozanne, from *Charts and Plates to La Pérouse's Voyage*, 1798.

for he claimed to have seen some Admiralty Islanders wearing French naval uniforms. D'Entrecasteaux would begin the search there, but decided to approach it via the south coast of Australia, where he made the important discovery of the harbour on which the city of Hobart, Tasmania, now stands. The discoveries made by the relief expedition surpassed those made by poor Lapérouse, while the charts of the south coast of Australia produced by D'Entrecasteux's civilian engineer, Beautemps-Beaupré, were models of their type and would be used extensively by Matthew Flinders in his survey of Australia in 1801–03. Beautemps-Beaupré later wrote a textbook on marine surveying which was translated into English in the 1820s and quickly supplanted the ones by Alexander Dalrymple and Murdoch McKenzie, which had been published in the 1770s and which had remained the only books available on the subject.

Over two seasons D'Entrecasteaux explored Hunter's theory and retraced as much as possible of Lapérouse's projected route, but he found no trace of the missing ships. In May 1793, they reached the Santa Cruz group seeing to the north of Santa Cruz itself an island that did not appear on any map: this they named Ile de la Recherche, after their ship, but sailed on without further investigation. It was the island of Vanikoro, where Lapérouse's ships had, in fact, been wrecked and it is even possible that two of the crew were still alive on the island when *Recherche* and *Espérance* passed by. D'Entrecasteaux's ships returned to France unable to shed any light on Lapérouse's disappearance, but the mystery remained in the public mind for years. D'Entrecasteaux's was the only official search expedition but every French voyage to the Pacific over the next thirty years would at the very least have Lapérouse in mind. As late as 1826, the instructions to the navigator Dumont D'Urville suggested that 'Your voyage will have added interest if you succeed in discovering traces of La Pérouse and his unfortunate companions.' By the time D'Urville reached the Pacific, however, the mystery had finally been solved.

In 1826, an Irish trader called Peter Dillon heard of an islander offering for sale a sword hilt of French design, which he had found on Vanikoro. Intrigued and mindful of the 10,000 francs reward offered way back in 1791 by the French government for news of Lapérouse, Dillon took the hilt with him to Calcutta where he managed to persuade the East India Company to let him lead a search expedition to the island. Once on Vanikoro he was able to buy a number of objects, clearly of European origin, which had come from a reef on the west coast of the island. He also learnt something of the fate of Lapérouse and his companions from questioning the islanders. The two ships, still sailing in company, had struck the reef during a cyclone. One ship had almost immediately broken up and the surviving crew were killed by islanders as they struggled ashore; the other stayed relatively intact and the crew was able to keep together as a group and build an encampment on the beach: Dillon was shown a large clearing which was supposed to be the site of the camp. This party managed to construct a boat from the timbers of their wrecked ship and, leaving two men behind on the island, they eventually sailed away to an unknown but imaginable fate. Dillon took the relics and his story to France, where an ageing Barthélémy de Lesseps confirmed that they belonged to the expedition. Dillon was received by the French king, Charles X, who ensured that he received his 10,000 francs, a government pension of 4000 francs a year and was made a Chevalier of the Légion d'Honneur. Dumont D'Urville arrived on Vanikoro four months after Dillon had left, in response to a message left for him in Hobart, but he was not able to add materially to the story, although he collected a few more artefacts and raised some guns from the wreck site. Over the next 150 years other expeditions and dives on the wrecks would find more objects. The anchors raised in 1883 adorn the statue to Lapérouse in his home town of Albi where, more recently, the Musée Lapérouse has opened.

The journals sent back from Kamchatka and Botany Bay were edited by an army officer, Baron de Milet-Mureu, and published in 1797 as part of an arrangement which would have provided a pension for Lapérouse's widow. But, incomplete, lacking most of the scientific observations which were the voyage's primary purpose, and with the expedition's fate still unknown, the book did not grasp the public imagination and was not a financial success. Lapérouse's achievements were, from the first, dominated by his disappearance in much the same way that Cook's third voyage was by his death on Hawaii. The achievements were, in fact, considerable, although necessarily diminished by the voyage's abrupt end.

Lapérouse consciously adopted many of the practices established by Cook, and with no little success: in just under three years he lost only one man to scurvy although, like Cook, he was no nearer to understanding the underlying causes of the disease. He used similar navigational and cartographical techniques to Cook and the resulting charts were produced to a high degree of accuracy: the shortcomings in the survey of the American coast were due largely to weather and lack of time. While most of the scientific data was lost with the shipwreck, what was sent back from Spanish America, Macao and Port Jackson was valuable and the indications are that, although Lapérouse undoubtedly had his problems with the civilian scientists, this did not affect the quality of their work. Perhaps the single most significant achievement was, as a recent French historian has observed, that 'Lapérouse ushered in the era of scientific navigation in France and played a role analogous to that represented by Cook in the history of exploration'. While his expedition can be seen as a continuation of an already well-established tradition of French maritime activity in the Pacific, of which Bougainville's voyage is the most well-known example, Lapérouse's was the first of a number of large, state-sponsored voyages which would make important contributions to Europe's knowledge of the Pacific. They would also eventually usher in colonization when Dupetit-Thouars annexed the Marquesas and Tahiti in the 1830s, laying the foundations of France's Pacific empire.

'Naufrage de l'Astrolabe', an imaginative depiction of the wreck of *Astrolabe* and *Boussole* on the rocks of Vanikoro. Hand-coloured lithograph by Louis LeBreton, who sailed as a surgeon on Dumont D'Urville's voyage, 1837–40.

CHAPTER FOUR

THE TRIALS OF CAPTAIN BLIGH

'Let our old Captain's frailties be forgotten & view him as a
man of Science and excellent practical seaman. He has
suffered much and ever in difficulty by labour and
perseverance extricated himself . . .'
– *George Tobin to Frank Bond, 15 December 1817*

Captain Cook's domination of Pacific exploration makes it easy to
overlook the group of younger talents who began their careers under him
as midshipmen, master's mates or in other capacities. George Vancouver is
covered elsewhere (see pp. 96–115) but, among others, Alexander Hood was
the nephew of celebrated admirals and became a captain at twenty-one,
dying heroically in a single-ship duel in 1798 and Edward Riou played a
small part in the Botany Bay story (see p. 38) before being killed under
Nelson at Copenhagen in 1801. Cook's own nephew, Isaac Smith, and James
Burney both rose to be admirals, the latter's importance as a historian of
Pacific exploration augmenting the fame of his otherwise artistically talented
family. James Trevenen saw much later action and died in Russian service
against the Swedes, after war forestalled him leading a Russian survey voyage
to the Bering Strait. Lastly here, the American-born Nathaniel Portlock,
along with George Dixon, *Discovery*'s armourer on the third voyage,
captained the two ships of the King George's Sound Company that
pioneered the British fur trade on the American north-west coast in
1785–88. They returned around the world, which Portlock circumnavigated a
third time on a voyage to transport breadfruit from Tahiti to the West Indies
in 1791–93. On this occasion it was as commander of the schooner *Assistant*
in the second 'breadfruit expedition' led by Cook's third-voyage sailing master
in *Resolution*, William Bligh. He is, of course, is best known for his first
attempt in the *Bounty*, which ended in a mid-Pacific mutiny in 1789. Cast
adrift, Bligh and eighteen companions were only saved by his own skills as a
seaman and navigator in a boat voyage to safety of more than 3600 miles.
Had they died – which was a far more likely outcome – we might now know
as little of the *Bounty* affair as we do of the disaster that overtook Lapérouse
at the same time on the reefs of Vanikoro.

Captain William Bligh, 1803. A fine
study in pencil and watercolour by
the miniaturist John Smart. It was
only finished as far as necessary
for engraving as one of eighteen
cameo portraits in a large print
commemorating the Battle of
Camperdown, 1797, where Bligh
distinguished himself as captain of
the *Director*.

Mutiny on the *Bounty*, 1787–89

Born on 9 September 1754, William Bligh came from an old Cornish family with naval, military, aristocratic and customs connections, his father being a Plymouth customs officer. He went to sea at the age of fifteen, rated as an able seaman (AB) until 1774 and midshipman thereafter, primarily learning his navigation and seamanship from three years (1771–74) in the 36-gun frigate *Crescent* in the West Indies, and two in the sloop *Ranger*. The latter was involved in anti-smuggling operations in the Irish Sea, based at Douglas in the Isle of Man, where he formed significant connections. It was at that point, when he was twenty-one, that Cook picked him as master of the *Resolution*, undoubtedly over more experienced men. This suggests that someone important recommended him, though Cook must also have been impressed by his journals and his charts, which Bligh would have submitted to the Admiralty. None of these survives from his pre-*Resolution* days, and he later stated that he lost all his own early charts from 1774 onward with the *Bounty*.

As master and the other principal surveyor, Bligh certainly worked closely with Cook. A number of his charts from the voyage are identifiable and whatever gloss he acquired from Cook as a navigator and surveyor he closely followed his shipboard regime on both the *Bounty* and *Providence* voyages. This included insistence on high standards of cleanliness in vessels and men, and on a good anti-scorbutic diet and exercise, however much sailors disliked 'greens' and enforced dancing for their health to a seaman fiddler (Bligh's innovation in *Bounty*, even though the man he chose was near-blind and of little other use). He also maintained Cook's then unusual practice of a three-watch system which allowed eight hours' rest in twelve rather than four on, four off. Less admirably, he would have seen Cook's occasional gesticulating outbursts of temper – his own being in similar style – which Cook's crews called his 'heivas', after a vigorous Tahitian dance.

Bligh's failing, though one that only the *Bounty*'s circumstances made critical, was to have a short fuse too much of the time. A cautious and often self-congratulatory perfectionist, he saw others' failures to meet the standards that he expected in both ends and means as worrying slackness. While 'placid and interesting' in private, on duty he switched from civility to invective with dizzying ease, though he was not physically brutal by contemporary standards. He was not an excessive 'flogger' either of his own men or of Tahitian thieves, finding it little deterrent in the latter case. Cook, by contrast, dealt more severely with native theft and had one inveterate culprit's ear cut off.

Bligh's genius – of which he seems to have remained unaware – was for inducing severe stress in subordinates who disappointed him, especially those lacking hardened maturity. The Navy did not recognize this critical weakness either, since it ran by clear rules, with no concept of 'psychological' mitigation to explain disobedience and failure of duty. Bligh's reputation was tarnished by what emerged about his style of command in the court martial of the *Bounty* mutineers – not least since he was by then again in the Pacific and unable to defend himself. However, the worst official reprimand that he ever had was as captain of the *Warrior* in 1805, when one of his lieutenants called him before a court martial for 'tyrannical behaviour'. The charge being partly upheld, he was simply reprimanded and told to moderate his language. It is more notable that while he was one of many captains turned out of their ships during the fleet mutiny at the Nore in 1797, when he was in command of the *Director*, he was not on the mutineers' blacklist of the hundred most unpopular officers, whom the Admiralty agreed to replace. Rather, he was well respected by his crew and defended them in the affair, blaming agitators who had come aboard from other ships. In short, his fitness to command was well within accepted norms and his competence as a seaman, navigator and careful husband of his men's welfare was exceptional. His volatility limited but did not stop his advancement and it was other exceptional circumstances that combined with it to spark the most famous of Royal Naval mutinies, in the *Bounty*. However, it was also one that was very untypical in being neither a fleet 'strike' nor a single-ship revolt against unarguable physical tyranny.

Signs of Bligh's ability to make himself unpopular appeared on *Resolution* after Cook's death on Hawaii in 1779. Both in the events surrounding that, and on the rest of the voyage, Bligh behaved with

Elizabeth Bligh, by John Russell, about 1790. This pastel portrait of Bligh's wife was done as a pair with one of him, both now at the Captain Cook Memorial Museum, Whitby. Bligh's was engraved in 1792, in his second and fuller published account of the *Bounty* voyage.

resolution and professional skill. However, he did not respect John Gore, on whom command of *Resolution* eventually devolved, and appears to have alienated Cook's second lieutenant, James King, who brought *Discovery* home in 1780. On return Gore, King and nearly every other officer was promoted, some less deserving than Bligh. He was not, presumably because Gore and King did not recommend him. King was in fact almost Bligh's antithesis in personality, as expert an astronomer as Bligh was a navigator, popular and 'one of the politest, genteelest & best-bred men in the world'. When he completed the official write-up of the voyage proceedings, Bligh was incensed to find that all charts included that were not Cook's were credited to Henry Roberts – another post-voyage 'promotee' who only made fair copies of Cook's and Bligh's surveys. That Bligh received a one-eighth share of the publication profits confirms his creative rights but King gave him no credit. Personal antipathy aside, the explanation probably lies in Bligh's private criticism of those accompanying Cook at his death and the absence of retribution for it. Lieutenant John Williamson's irresolution in

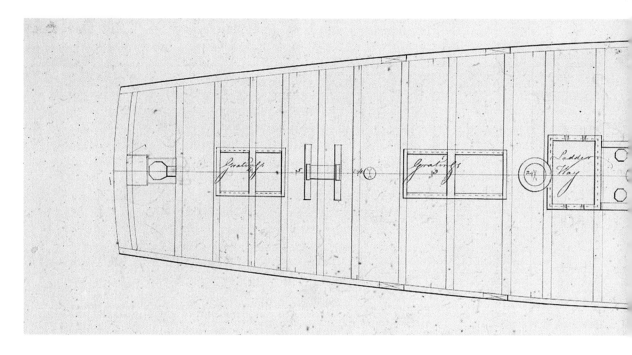

the matter was notorious but even he was promoted, only to have his cowardice confirmed by court martial after the Battle of Camperdown in 1797, where he commanded the *Agincourt*. Bligh, by contrast, showed his courage there and had probably approached the *Bounty* voyage ten years earlier with some bitter memories and a point to prove.

In February 1781, at Douglas in the Isle of Man, Bligh began a happy thirty-year marriage to Elizabeth Betham, intelligent daughter of Richard Betham LL.D, the Receiver General of Customs there, and two weeks later was appointed master of the frigate *Belle Poule* in the North Sea. That August he fought in the Battle of the Dogger Bank, against the Dutch, after which he was at last promoted to lieutenant, briefly in the *Berwick* and *Princess Amelia*, and then as sixth lieutenant of the *Cambridge* in March 1782. *Cambridge* took part in Lord Howe's relief of Gibraltar from Spanish siege later in the year but was paid off at the war's end in January 1783. Bligh returned to his 'Betsy' and daughter Harriet (the first of six) at Douglas, but needed more than his half-pay to support them. Fortunately his wife's uncle was Duncan Campbell, a shipowner and the government contractor for the recently introduced prison-hulk system (see p. 22). For the next four years Bligh gained profitable experience as a merchant captain commanding three of Campbell's West Indian traders as well as acting as his agent in Jamaica. It was in Campbell's *Britannia* in 1787 that he was persuaded to take on a well-educated and ambitious volunteer midshipman, of Cumbrian origin and Manx residence. This was Fletcher Christian, who had only previously sailed in the frigate *Eurydice*.

While Bligh and Christian made two voyages together in *Britannia* and became ill-fated friends, a plan was evolving in London to transplant

Deck plans of the *Bounty*. The three deck plans were drawn on a single sheet at the time of her conversion in 1787. This is the flush upper deck, the others below it on the sheet are shown on pp. 64-5 and pp. 66-7.

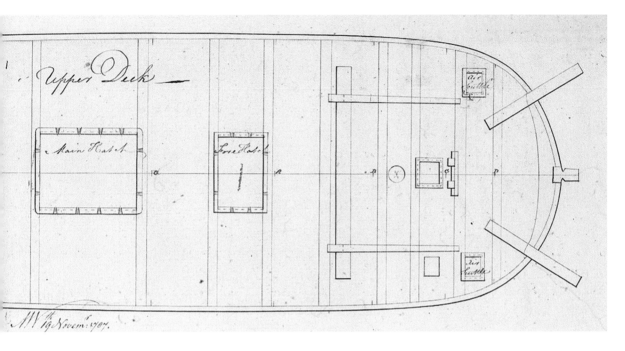

breadfruit, a staple of the Tahitian diet, to the West Indies as a cheap food for plantation slaves. Cook's voyages had made the plant well known, notably to Joseph Banks on the *Endeavour* voyage, who was now President of the Royal Society. In May 1787 George III instructed Lord Sydney to issue orders for the Admiralty to allocate a ship to the experiment. The small vessel provided, the consequently inadequate command structure and deficient planning – none the fault of Bligh – indicated that the Navy was less than enthusiastic. It was, however, a great opportunity for a suitable junior officer and Bligh's name probably came up early given his Pacific and West Indian experience, with Campbell certainly lobbying Banks on his behalf. On his return in the *Britannia* in August 1787 it was Banks whom he thanked for his 'great goodness' in honouring him with the command, even before the Admiralty confirmed it.

By then the Navy Board had already purchased a ship and was fitting her out. They had also been told to choose one no larger than 250 tons and, in the event, the selection fell to Banks and David Nelson, the senior gardener for the voyage, who had also sailed on Cook's last expedition. This ensured suitability for plants but not for other factors that might have given pause to an experienced seaman like Bligh. The choice, a 215-ton West Indiaman called *Bethia* but now renamed *Bounty* was in fact the smallest vessel considered. That was very small for the nature of her mission and a passage prescribed to be 'west-about' to Tahiti, on the shortest route via Cape Horn. From there orders also directed her to circumnavigate westward, making up any breadfruit losses with other exotic plants from the East Indies.

By contrast, the solid *Endeavour* was of 368 tons and, after nearly

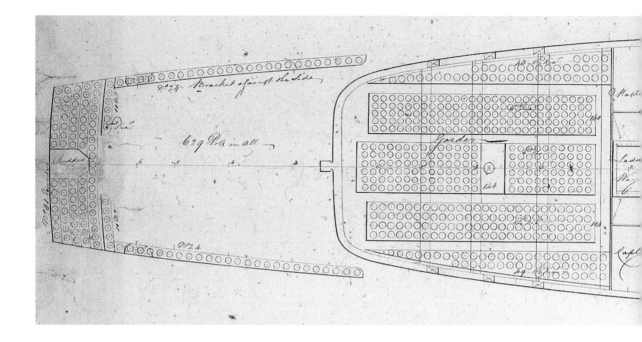

losing her on the Great Barrier Reef, Cook never again sailed with just one ship. Of these the *Discovery*, at 299 tons, was the smallest and *Resolution* the largest, at 462 tons. After the *Endeavour* voyage, Cook also never again risked the hazards and delays of beating west round Cape Horn. Instead he took the longer route east before the prevailing winds from the Cape of Good Hope, and used New Zealand harbours as his base for launching out into the Pacific.

The size of 'His Majesty's armed vessel *Bounty*' also defined her as a 'cutter', the smallest of vessels, for complement. This rated only a lieutenant in command, no other commissioned officers who would have buttressed Bligh's authority and no Marines to defend it or the ship. These were all advantages that Cook enjoyed even when only a lieutenant commanding the *Endeavour*, which, like all his larger vessels, was rated as a 'sloop'. Bligh himself, Banks and others canvassed for his promotion to rectify this situation: Lord Howe at the Admiralty refused.

Bligh had never been round the Horn either way, so the deficiencies deriving from both choice of ship and prescribed route lay not with him but the Admiralty, which then compounded normal delays by an unaccountable one of three weeks in issuing sailing orders. This almost guaranteed adverse weather at the Horn. Despite heroic efforts, Bligh could not beat into the Pacific and was forced to turn back the long way round via the Indian Ocean, for which he only had contingency permission. Arriving well behind schedule at Tahiti, it then took time to get plants ready and wait to catch seasonal winds for the return voyage. The exhausting outward struggle with the Horn and incidents on the long following passage sapped crew morale in one way, over-long dalliance in

Lower-deck plan of the *Bounty*. This shows how the great cabin was to be used on the return voyage, given over to racks holding 692 pots of breadfruit plants, leaving no communal space for Bligh's officers.

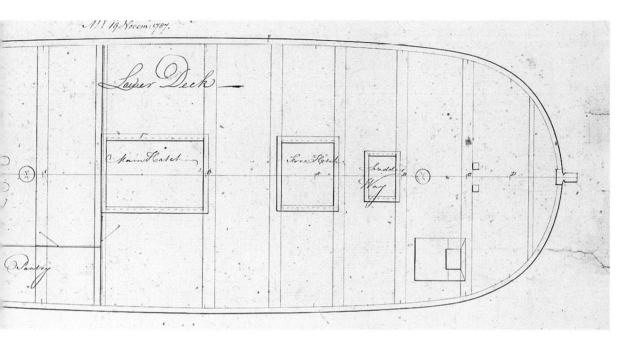

an aphrodisiacal South Sea paradise undermined discipline in another. Other factors also raised the odds on trouble.

Bounty's crew was the usual mixture of the reliable, the indifferent, the immature and some confirmed troublemakers. Good men included the armourer John Coleman, the gunner William Peckover and the sailmaker, Lawrence Lebogue. Peckover spoke Tahitian, having sailed on all three of Cook's voyages, while Lebogue – at forty, one of the oldest men in the ship – had been under Bligh in the *Britannia* and would sail with him again in the *Providence*. Some of the hard cases were Charles Churchill, the violent and unpopular ship's corporal, James Morrison, bosun's mate, and ABs Matthew Quintal, John Williams and 'Alexander Smith' – whose real name was John Adams. Williams was the first of the mutineers to die on Pitcairn Island; Adams survived easily the longest, dying in 1829. William Purcell, the carpenter, proved corrosively insubordinate from an early stage but drew the line between that and mutiny. John Fryer, the master, was competent but soon became anxious and resentful as Bligh's greater competence and censorious style undermined his role, while the surgeon, Thomas Huggan, was a slovenly alcoholic. The meticulous Bligh tried unsuccessfully to shed him before the voyage, during which his growing incapacity proved both dangerous and a standing affront to good discipline.

Of a complement of forty-four under Bligh, twenty-five would be implicated in the mutiny: two, Churchill and Matthew Thompson, were later killed on Tahiti and four died as captives in the wreck of the pursuing *Pandora*, whose captain, Edward Edwards, carried off guilty and innocent with equal severity when he found them there in 1791. Nine were eventually tried in 1792. Three, including the loyal Coleman, were acquitted as uninvolved and six sentenced to hang, though only three 'foot-soldiers' were in fact executed. Those pardoned included the plausible Morrison and the gentlemanly Manxman Peter Heywood, whom Bligh had been pressed to take as a fifteen-year-old midshipman by his wife's father. Heywood, who later rose to be a naval captain, would have hanged less for active mutiny – his role remaining somewhat equivocal – than for failure to distance himself clearly from it, and owed his salvation to being both well defended and well connected. The remaining fourteen, including another gentleman AB, Edward Young, would vanish with *Bounty* herself to a mostly violent fate on remote Pitcairn under their leader, Fletcher Christian. Christian was only twenty-four when he finally cracked after a trivial row over missing coconuts (Bligh claimed they had been stolen) that involved several of the officers. With the accumulated effects of his captain's temper, Tahiti and the suicidal loss of self-esteem that failing to meet his own and Bligh's expectations seems to have induced, this was the last straw for Christian.

Bligh finally sailed from Portsmouth, into bad weather, on 23 December 1787 and on 5 January put into Tenerife. Shortly afterwards he began his three-watch system but needed a third watch-keeping officer in addition to Fryer and Peckover. For this he picked his protégé Christian, then a master's mate, and early in March rapidly advanced him to acting lieutenant – a rank the Admiralty would customarily have confirmed on return. Compared to the thirty-three-year-old Bligh – and to Fryer, who probably resented the favouritism – he was very inexperienced, and, though he knew Bligh to be 'passionate', flattered himself he could deal with this. In the event both men had unrealistic hopes: Bligh's disillusionment with Christian and the gradual psychological disintegration that his expression of it induced had a devastating finale. 'I am in hell' was the sole, hopelessly inarticulate explanation that the latter could give his astonished mentor when he cast him adrift.

Bounty reached Cape Horn in the last week of March, the start of the southern autumn, and for a month Bligh tried to fight his way round against huge seas and westerly gales before turning for the Cape of Good Hope. That his crew sustained the struggle so long was remarkable, since only thirteen of those rated as 'able-bodied' (of which his complement was nominally twenty-five) were in fact mature seamen. They were greatly helped by Bligh's well-organized regime in which hot food was regularly provided and clothes systematically dried in the galley. He in turn was proud to reach Cape Town still with a crew free of 'scurvy, flux or fever' and no deaths or serious injuries. *Bounty* sailed again on 1 July 1788, east for Tahiti, though Bligh also took aboard seeds and fruit plants for Governor Phillip's nascent colony at Botany Bay, in case he accidentally landed up there. Instead, they had a tedious but rough passage straight to Adventure Bay, Tasmania. Here the first unusual disciplinary incident of the voyage occurred, when William Purcell twice refused to comply with Bligh's orders concerning wooding and watering ashore. Exactly why this

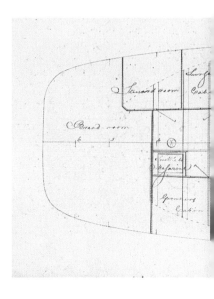

Hold plan of the *Bounty*, with officers' cabins fore and aft and the hold in the middle.

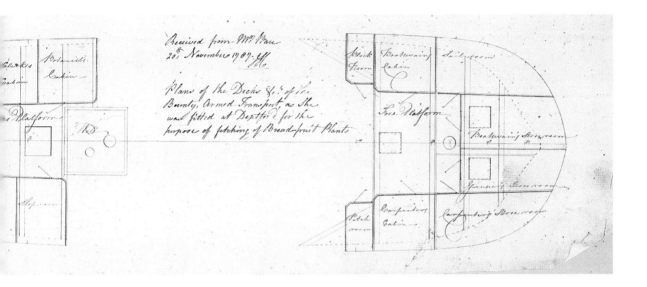

happened is unknown: Purcell claimed that the work was not proper to his carpenter's rating but Bligh could neither keep so vital a craftsman confined until later court martial nor flog him, warrant officers being exempt from such punishment. Purcell returned to his senses when Bligh told him that no work meant no food but, effectively, unpunished defiance of orders was a serious challenge to Bligh's authority.

The breach was widened shortly afterwards by Fryer, who refused to countersign Bligh's audit of Purcell's and Cole's regular accounts without Bligh certifying Fryer's own satisfactory performance. Bligh forced his retreat by reading out the Articles of War and the master's standing instructions before the ship's company. However, it was another extraordinary incident, probably indirectly connected with the death of James Valentine, a seaman, from septicaemia caused by the incompetence of the drunken surgeon, Huggan. Bligh was not satisfied with Fryer and the master should also have been aware of Valentine's condition, Bligh having been made to understand he was recovering. Huggan compounded his ineptitude before Tahiti, first by misdiagnosing scurvy in several men – which incensed Bligh as much as scurvy itself would have after all his precautions – and then by wrongly certifying the crew clear of venereal disease. After final reasoning had failed, Bligh had the surgeon's filthy berth cleaned and his liquor supplies confiscated, though not permanently enough to prevent his alcoholic death in December 1788 at Matavai Bay.

Here they had arrived on 26 October and renewed friendly contact with the local chief Tinah, well known to Cook in his earlier name of Tu or Otoo. Following Cook's example, Bligh issued strict orders to prevent native theft and maintain the value of trade exchange through a single official 'trader', a task given to the Tahitian-speaking Peckover. He also forbade theft or the violent recovery of stolen items from the Tahitians, and any maltreatment of them especially with firearms: these were only to be used where life was threatened. The arrival of *Bounty* was an opportunity for Tinah to reassert himself following ill fortune in recent local conflict. Bligh had brought many gifts and rapidly secured as many breadfruit plants as he wished for 'King George' in return. When he later said he might move on to other islands, Tinah offered to supply all needs rather than see him go. This suited Bligh well and the only move, at Christmas, was along the coast to the more sheltered anchorage of Oparre. In both places Christian took charge of the shore camp and Fryer of the ship, with Bligh coming and going in close and inevitably critical supervision. Many of the crew, including Fryer – but not Bligh any more than Cook – formed liaisons with local women for the duration. Christian's seem to have been unspecific until after the mutiny, when his Tahitian 'Isabella' (the mother of his son, Thursday) accompanied him to Pitcairn. Fryer later caused trouble by misappropriating property of his lover, one of several incidents of casual attitudes to local sensibilities which Bligh had to counter.

Peter Heywood (1773–1831) by John Simpson, 1822. As a midshipman on the *Bounty*, Heywood's part in the mutiny was confused but he stayed on the ship as far as Tahiti, where he was seized by the *Pandora*. He was later sentenced to death as a mutineer but powerful connections won his pardon and return to service. He is shown here as a naval captain, the rank he held when he retired in 1813.

Native theft was a more immediate problem, Bligh's most effective countermeasure being to punish his own men for the carelessness that usually caused the losses. For seamen (such as Adams, alias Smith, on 4 November) this meant flogging, for the officers a lashing with his tongue. Before long, Purcell again stood on the strict letter of his duty, defied a reasonable request of Bligh's and was only briefly confined, while Thompson, a seaman, received twelve lashes for equal 'insolence and disobedience'. By contrast, Coleman earned Bligh's praise for his readiness to help Tahitians by forging useful items from pieces of iron brought to him. For Fryer and Christian, the move to Oparre coincided with a decline in Bligh's opinion of both. Fryer, having surveyed the channel, managed to run the ship aground in it by keeping a poor lookout, while Christian, in the ship's launch, also failed to stay on station ahead to prevent this. Bligh was probably incandescent at such bungling of a simple manoeuvre. Fryer and Cole were later to incur his wrath when sails were taken from store and found to be mouldy through lack of proper care, a matter well within Fryer's supervisory remit. Bligh recorded that he would have replaced both men had the option existed. Fryer later also let the ship's indispensable timekeeper run down because he forgot to wind it. (This was Kendall's second official copy of Harrison's great prototype: the first, used by Cook, was then with Arthur Phillip in Australia.)

On 5 January 1789, a week after arriving at Oparre, desertions finally started to occur – a potentially capital offence but one already known in the Pacific. The absconders in *Bounty*'s small cutter were Churchill, William Muspratt – recently flogged for 'neglect of duty' – and John Milward. A paper found in Churchill's possessions also named three of the shore party, including Christian, though Bligh accepted their denials that they were aware of what this implied. Fryer then blundered by not detaining a Tahitian who came on board and admitted to helping the deserters but on 23 January all three were recaptured. They were put in irons and flogged. All expressed contrition and gratitude for the leniency, being aware that later court martial would have delivered worse. At the end of their stay a particularly bad case of Tahitian theft earned the culprit one hundred lashes. Although by far the heaviest beating Bligh ordered, its severity was partly to counter the unacceptable urgings of local chiefs that the culprit be killed when they delivered him up. The man bore it with apparent indifference.

Bounty at last sailed for the East Indies on 4 March 1789 with more than 700 breadfruit plants potted up in racks in her great cabin, and stuffed with supplies of local produce, pigs and goats, as well as private stores and curiosities of all kinds. The farewells were ceremonious and affectionate, but also distressing to many couples about to be separated. Christian's party, especially, now found itself back in the confinement of the ship under Bligh's immediate management, after twenty-three easier weeks ashore.

Things finally came to a head at Annamooka in Tonga on 24–26 April

where Christian, master's mate William Elphinstone and Fryer went ashore with parties to collect wood and water. The result was a spate of native thefts arising from the fact that local chiefs were not immediately on hand, the inexperience of dealing with islanders less easily controlled than the Tahitians, and Bligh's orders against the use of firearms. Bligh appears to have damned Christian publicly as a 'cowardly rascal' in the matter and Morrison later recalled that at their departure he berated the assembled crew as a 'parcel of lubberly rascals', pointing a pistol at William McCoy and threatening to shoot him for inattention. The last flare-up was at sea on the 27th, with the coconut incident, in which Bligh exploded against several of the officers for at least winking at the apparent theft of these supplies, although Christian was only cast in the role of principal victim in accounts written by his subsequent apologists.

By now Bligh clearly considered all his officers lax and again told them so in no uncertain terms. The tempest over he then typically forgot the matter and asked Christian to dine with him. He declined and, as night

'The Mutineers turning Liett. Bligh and part of the Officers and Crew adrift from His Majesty's Ship the Bounty', painted and engraved by Robert Dodd in London, 1790. This is the most famous image of the *Bounty* mutiny but it is only a reconstruction. Bligh is the standing figure without a coat. Two mutineers are throwing swords and clothing into the boat from the stern windows, above which stand Christian and other armed mutineers.

fell, finally succumbed to the private 'hell' boiling in his head since Annamooka. He first contemplated suicide, then swimming to Tofoa, thirty miles away. This developed into an equally wild plan to escape on a makeshift raft, about which he spoke to several people. One he confided in was Midshipman George Stewart, who later died in *Pandora*. Stewart dissuaded him, saying the crew were 'ripe for anything', and this seems to have lit the fuse of mutiny.

After a fitful sleep Christian came on watch at 4 a.m., rapidly recruited Quintal and he in turn the violent duo of Churchill and Thompson. Smith (Adams), McCoy and John Williams also joined and, thanks to Fryer's lax procedures, Christian easily obtained the key to the arms locker from the unsuspecting armourer, Coleman. At daybreak on 28 April 1789, the sleeping Bligh was seized in his bed by Christian and three others, tied up and lashed to the mizzen mast on deck. Fryer was also detained.

In the ensuing hours of chaos, it soon became clear that, while the core of armed mutineers were united and determined, they could only recruit just over half the remaining crew. No one was prepared to kill Bligh and in the end he and eighteen men – the most it could hold, including Fryer and Purcell – were cast adrift in the ship's 23-foot launch. *Bounty* then vanished forever, eventually to remote and mischarted Pitcairn. By 1808, when Captain Mayhew Folger of the American whaler *Topaz* landed there, only John Adams remained, benign patriarch of a community of twenty-six English-speaking mutineers' children and eight of their Tahitian mothers. All the other mutineers and their few Tahitian male companions had long since died, mostly through internecine killings. One such had accounted for Christian in 1793, after *Bounty* herself was stripped and burnt in 1790 to preclude detection, including by further flight.

The voyage of the *Bounty*'s launch
Those left in the boat should also have died, as the mutineers expected them to. However, 150 pounds of ship's biscuit, 28 gallons of water, a little pork, rum, wine, coconuts and breadfruit were put aboard in the mêlée, with clothes and Purcell's tools, Bligh's papers and basic navigational items including tables and a sextant. Bligh immediately headed for nearby Tofoa where they foraged with only limited success from 29 April to 2 May. The boat held no firearms, something quickly observed by natives who arrived on the 1st and, with easy pickings in view, attacked the following day. Bligh saw it coming and just managed to get the boat away with the loss of a sturdy loyalist, John Norton, who was killed on the beach. In the shocked aftermath it was clear to all that without guns they were unlikely to be better treated elsewhere. Bligh therefore set sail for Dutch Timor in the East Indies, more than 3600 miles to the west, having extracted a solemn oath from all to abide by the most stringent rationing of their supplies. These were initially an ounce of bread (biscuit) a day but later reduced and supplemented until they reached Australia only by a couple of birds eaten raw.

John Adams, alias Alexander Smith. One of the more violent mutineers and their last survivor on Pitcairn Island. He died there aged about sixty-seven in 1829, as Christian patriarch of the 'Anglo-Tahitian' community they had created. This print is from a drawing by Midshipman Richard Beechey of HMS *Blossom*, which called at Pitcairn in 1825.

The voyage that followed was Bligh's finest. The launch was down to within inches of the water and in stormy and often torrentially rainy weather staying afloat required skill and endlessly exhausting bailing. Everyone was perpetually cold, wet, often terrified, and only able to sleep fitfully in the exposed and cramped conditions. Bligh had no charts and only his memory of the south-west Pacific to go on, but none the less managed to plot an accurate course in a small notebook, using an improvised log line, latitude observations and Peckover's watch. This kept going until 2 June, albeit not as accurately as *Bounty*'s chronometer (which went to Pitcairn). Early on they were pursued by two canoes but escaped and did not attempt to land again until Bligh predicted that they were approaching the northern Barrier Reef. On 29 May they landed within it on what Bligh called Restoration Island. Here stress-induced disagreements broke out again followed by a blazing row further up the coast, when some men – admittedly weakened – refused to help to forage on Sunday Island. Purcell was again insolent and Fryer, attempting to defuse the situation, appeared to side with him when Bligh threatened Purcell with a cutlass. At this point Bligh noted only ten men he felt he

Coconut cup, horn beaker and bullet weight (one-twenty-fifth of a pound) used during the voyage of the *Bounty*'s launch, 28 April–14 June 1789, after the mutiny. The cup bears Bligh's inscription, partly cut and partly in ink: 'W Bligh / April 1789 / The cup I eat my miserable allowance out.' The beaker once bore his note: 'Allowance of water 3 times a day'. The bullet's later silver mount records its use to weigh out the thrice daily bread allowance to the men in the boat.

The *Bounty*'s launch. A modern 1:48 scale model from the original official plans. The 23-foot (7-metre) launch carried nineteen men (including Bligh) a distance of 3618 nautical miles in forty-one days' sailing from off Tofoa to Timor in the Dutch East Indies. It remains the greatest-ever voyage of survival in an open-boat.

could rely on, Fryer and Purcell being among those he could not.

By 4 June they were again at sea north of Cape York but, despite the brief respite, Lebogue and Ledward, the assistant surgeon, were seen to be sinking fast. It was therefore with 'an excess of joy' that early on 12 June they sighted Timor, though another dispute rapidly ensued between Bligh and Fryer about the former's decision to seek a European harbour rather than first get ashore for more food. Finally, on 14 June the launch made port at Coupang, the Dutch colonial island's capital, where they were well received and cared for by the authorities. It was the forty-eighth day since the mutiny. The party had suffered no deaths from exposure or starvation, though Nelson, the gardener, and another man died shortly afterwards from local fevers, as did three others before they reached home.

Arrival did not close the factional breach, however, which came to its last crisis at Sourabaya that September. Bligh and his men arrived there *en route* to Batavia, in a schooner that he bought on credit at Coupang and named *Resource*. On the point of leaving he found several men incapable of work and asked Fryer if they were ill (they were in fact drunk). On receiving an insolent reply, followed by general complaints about ill usage from others including Purcell, Bligh this time reached for a bayonet before calling in the Dutch authorities to support him. In the ensuing local inquiry no one laid a serious complaint against Bligh although Fryer renewed charges of financial impropriety. He subsequently withdrew these when Bligh produced his accounts.

Bligh later had Purcell tried for insubordination, for which the carpenter was reprimanded but he laid no formal complaints against Fryer, although they would have been justified. Likewise, neither Fryer nor Purcell ever complained officially against Bligh. Unlike Christian, all three were tough and understood the unwritten rules. One mutiny was bad enough: more could ruin all concerned, irrespective of which side they had taken.

At Batavia the fractious company parted, Bligh reaching home on a Dutch ship with his clerk, John Samuel, and another loyal man in March 1790. On his return he rapidly published a preliminary account of the *Bounty*'s loss and his open-boat voyage as part of a campaign to secure his position. Lacking self-awareness of his own contribution to the mutiny he blamed the corrupting effect of Tahiti on evil men. Hearing no contrary view, the subsequent court martial for the loss of the *Bounty*, which Bligh and the men he saved faced in October, similarly absolved them all from blame.

K2, 'the *Bounty* watch'. This is Larcum Kendall's second copy (1771) of Harrison's epoch-making H4 chronometer. Taken on the *Bounty* it went with the mutineers to Pitcairn and, by a tortuous route, only came back to Britain in the 1840s.

The second breadfruit voyage, 1791–93

With his published account making him a celebrity, Bligh was rapidly promoted to commander, and then to captain in December. Four months later, on 16 April 1791, he was formally appointed to the new, 420-ton *Providence* to repeat the *Bounty* project of transplanting breadfruit to the West Indies, with a 500-guinea gratuity from the Jamaica Assembly to speed him. This time he selected the ship, only launched on 23 April, and had the 100-ton *Assistant* as consort. She was commanded by Lieutenant Portlock, promoted from master's mate in 1780 after bringing home *Resolution*'s advance despatches from Cape Town.

The *Providence* voyage shows similarities and differences with its predecessor. Events in the *Bounty* obscure the fact that, for all his troubles, Bligh was an important observer of the geography, society and natural history of everywhere he visited – Tahiti, the East Indies and the Cape of Good Hope. As he explained

'Lieut. Bligh and his Crew of the Ship Bounty hospitably received by the Governor of Timor' at the end of the launch voyage. Engraving by William Bromley after Peter Benazech.

to Banks, speaking of the *Bounty*'s launch, 'I have endeavoured to make the remaining part of my voyage of some avail even in my distress'd situation', and he kept a running survey through the Fiji islands, up the coast of Australia, through the Prince of Wales Islands off Cape York, and only avoided New Guinea for lack of firearms. This observation continued in *Providence*. It included discoveries round Adventure Bay, Tasmania, and a swift but competent recording of the Fiji islands on the westward passage from Tahiti. Perhaps the most remarkable achievement was a hazardous nineteen-day survey through the Clarence Islands of the Torres Strait, punctuated by two native attacks, in which one man died.

However, the essential difference between the two breadfruit voyages was that Bligh's advice underlay all preparations for the second, which reflected his customary foresight and the example set by Cook: two ships and a sound command structure, with a full complement of subordinate commissioned officers and a party of twenty-four Marines, four being in *Assistant*. Once at sea he also reinstituted the three-watch system and the same tight regime as in the *Bounty* for welfare and good order, both afloat and ashore. His irascibility when subordinates failed to meet his exacting standards was otherwise the same, not least since his own health was bad throughout the voyage as a result of the hardships he had already suffered. Young Matthew Flinders, who sailed with him, came to admire but never to like him and the old difficulties soon showed themselves again in Bligh's relationship with Francis Godolphin Bond, *Providence*'s first lieutenant.

Frank Bond was Bligh's nephew and already a lieutenant with long sea experience when Bligh invited his participation, so as to help his nephew's career. When Bond agreed, Bligh exerted influence to have him appointed but it was typical that, once aboard, considerate Uncle William became nagging and imperious Captain Bligh. This made the voyage a bitterly remembered purgatory for Bond, whose more easy-going outlook was bound to infuriate his uncle.

Consequently, and knowing his uncle's prior reputation as a 'tyrant', he soon had experience of his 'ungovernable temper' but was wise enough to conceal his resentment, of which Bligh remained unaware. By contrast, the sensible and artistic George Tobin, making his first commissioned voyage as the third lieutenant, recognized in Bligh 'the quickest sailor's eye, guided by a thorough knowledge of every branch of the profession necessary on such a voyage'. While Tobin's inexperience occasionally brought out 'the Unbridled licence of [Bligh's] power of Speech, yet [it was] never without soon receiving something like an emollient plaister to heal the wound' and he rapidly learnt how diligence avoided what he called 'passing squalls'. At the top end of the scale the experienced Portlock, in the *Assistant*, had a highly successful partnership with his leader. At Tahiti Bligh noted that his 'alertness and attention to duty makes me at all times think of him with regard and esteem', a unique encomium on any of his subordinates.

The ships sailed on 3 August 1791, east via Cape Town to Tasmania and thence direct to Tahiti, where they arrived on 9 April 1792. Here

Bligh discovered that *Bounty* had twice returned before vanishing, leaving the party that Edwards had already swept up. On 20 July, with 2126 breadfruit and about 500 other plants on board, Bligh left Tahiti again for the Torres Strait and Coupang, where he learnt a little of the fate of *Pandora* on the Barrier Reef. Mangoes were among other plants that he collected in the Indies and was thereby responsible for successfully introducing to the Caribbean, whither he sailed on the long westward passage via St Helena. He reached St Vincent on 23 January 1793 and went on to Jamaica, breadfruit being landed in both places. After all the trouble, however, it proved unpopular with the African slaves it was meant to feed but Bligh and Portlock received a warm welcome and generous rewards for their efforts from the authorities of both islands.

Nathaniel Portlock (1747–1817), artist unknown. Born in Virginia he served as a master's mate on Cook's last voyage and commanded the *Assistant* on Bligh's second breadfruit expedition. This portrait shows him as a merchant captain on his fur-trading voyage to north-west America (1785–88), bartering with a local man. His ship, *King George*, and her consort, *Queen Charlotte*, can be seen in the background.

They arrived home in August 1793 with a further cargo of West Indian plants for Kew Gardens but to rather less of a welcome. The country was already eight months into war with Revolutionary France and Bligh found his earlier fame soured by notoriety from the trial, in his absence, of the *Bounty* mutineers whom Edwards had brought home. Although the *Providence* expedition ended with complete success and, taken overall, considerable good feeling towards Bligh from his men, the Admiralty granted none of his officers their hoped-for promotions. Bligh himself was much later (1801) elected a Fellow of the Royal Society for his 'distinguished services to navigation' but in 1793–94 found himself writing a defensive pamphlet to rebut allegations made against him in connection with the mutineers' trial. The popular myth of 'wicked Captain Bligh' was well planted there while his back was turned and it has often needed cutting back to see Bligh the man in his true proportion ever since.

Rebellion, resistance and retirement

Bligh's last mutiny – more a *coup d'état* – which deposed him as Governor of New South Wales, owed something to his personality but little in the way of blame. In this case his assertive rectitude lacked subtlety but helped to end a situation too long out of control under his immediate naval predecessors, John Hunter from 1795 and Philip Gidley King from 1800.

Bligh was appointed governor in April 1805 though he only sailed for

Australia, accompanied by his daughter Mary, in February 1806. By this time his reputation for having a bad temper was augmented by one as a brave fighting commander. He distinguished himself as captain of the *Director* in Admiral Duncan's victory over the Dutch at Camperdown in 1797 and commanded the *Glatton* at the Battle of Copenhagen in 1801, fighting next in line astern to Nelson's *Elephant* and winning warm praise from him. His later command of the *Warrior* followed a brief spell of survey work in 1803–04, which included being temporarily in charge of the Hydrographic Office, and he only gave up her captaincy when Banks – and a generous salary – persuaded him to go to Australia.

The colony at Sydney Cove was by then firmly in the grip of the New South Wales Corps, notably that of the able but unscrupulous figure of the 'Perturbator', (now Captain) John Macarthur, a complex, depressive man of 'restless, ambitious and litigious disposition', in Hunter's phrase. This was complicated by conflicts between the officers of the Corps; between the Corps, the emancipated convicts and free settlers whom they exploited commercially; and between the Corps' private-property interests and its official role to support the authority of the Naval Governors after Arthur Phillip – a case of 'who will guard the guards' with inter-service discord thrown in. In the three-year interregnum between Phillip's departure and the return of Hunter, the Corps had subverted civil government, control of landholding, convict labour and trade through Sydney to its own profit – with Macarthur at the centre of the web as Regimental Paymaster from 1792 and Inspector of Public Works the following year. Both Hunter and King were well aware of the problem but unable to deal with it and were duly recalled as this became apparent. London also did not help in other ways. In 1801 Macarthur was sent home to face court martial for duelling with his commanding officer, Lieutenant-Colonel Paterson. However, the charge was dismissed in England where Macarthur also used the occasion to win substantial official support for an Australian wool-farming experiment, despite falling foul of Joseph Banks, and sailed for Sydney again in 1804 taking merino sheep with him. When the government shortly afterwards sought a replacement for King who was incorrupt, resourcefully independent, firm and 'not subject to whimper and whine when severity in discipline is wanted' Banks had just the man in mind and Bligh was appointed.

He reached Australia in late 1806, by which time Macarthur had evaded a new ban on Corps officers being involved in trade by resigning, and purported instead to represent the 'free inhabitants' – though Bligh quickly found this was not the case. Being well experienced in mercantile finance, and with no reason to favour Macarthur, he soon acquired a clear picture of his self-interests and baleful influence. He also found that, prohibitions or not, the Corps was thoroughly corrupt. His conclusion was that the whole Corps should be sent home and replaced, a view which threatened the military interest on which his own practical authority rested.

The complex outcome was that by January 1808 Macarthur had manipulated a commercial court case brought against him by another of his enemies, the colony's judge advocate, Richard Atkins, to make it a means of undermining Bligh. The aim was to provoke Bligh to take Atkins's part and Bligh duly fell into the trap, thereby demonstrating an improper bias to which the other six court officers formally objected, as Macarthur had intended. Bligh then ordered them to surrender their papers in the case and explain themselves before him. Macarthur easily presented this as an illegal ultimatum and, with other allies, petitioned Major George Johnston, commander of the Corps – and well aware of what was going on – to rescue the colony from Bligh's usurpation by arresting and supplanting him. This was ostentatiously done on 27 January 1808 leaving both Macarthur and Johnston in control until July when Lieutenant-Colonel Joseph Foveaux – another appalling and self-interested Corps officer – returned from London as Bligh's lieutenant-governor but also refused to reinstate him.

The 'rum rebellion' quickly fragmented into faction, during which Bligh remained under arrest for the next year at Government House, refusing to return home until London ordered him to. In January 1809, when Paterson returned as senior officer to Sydney, Bligh obtained permission to transfer into HMS *Porpoise*, which had come out with him three years earlier. As a ruse, he gave his word to sail immediately for London, breaking it once aboard, where his naval authority was unchallenged. Although Johnston and Macarthur left for London in March to prepare their cases, Bligh stayed at sea between Tasmania and the Sydney coast for another year, intercepting ships from home for intelligence and to revictual. His daughter Mary, married and widowed since their arrival in 1806, also remained with him ashore and afloat from the time of his arrest.

In 1809 London at last took decisive action by sending out the 73rd Regiment under Lieutenant-Colonel Lachlan Macquarie. He was also ordered to succeed Bligh as governor after formally reinstating him to reaffirm London's sole right to appoint and dismiss. This was not practical as Bligh was off Tasmania when Macquarie arrived on 28 December 1809 but he was none the less greeted with proper honours when he landed at Sydney again on 17 January 1810. Macquarie later wrote privately of him as 'most disagreeable [and] ... a very improper Person to be employed in any situation of Trust or Command and ... generally detested ...'. This harsh opinion clearly has some truth. However, it probably does not take sufficient account of the stress Bligh had then been under for two years and the fact that he certainly still had respectable support in Sydney.

Bligh finally left in the *Hindostan* on 12 May 1810, in a small convoy that carried away the whole 'Rum Corps' to become the British 102nd Regiment of Foot, but this time without his daughter. She had what can only have

John Macarthur (1766–1834), by an unknown artist. Known as the 'Perturbator', Macarthur was a rapacious and subversive trouble-maker in Australia from his arrival as a lieutenant in the New South Wales Corps in 1789. He was forced to return to England between 1809 and 1817.

been a whirlwind romance with Macquarie's deputy, Lieutenant-Colonel O'Donnell, and assured her bewildered father that she wished to marry him and stay in Australia. Although Bligh was soon persuaded, it must have been with mixed feelings that he gave her away in marriage for the second time just before he sailed, at a ceremony in Government House.

He returned to England and the rest of his family in October 1810. In May 1811, George Johnston, now lieutenant-colonel of the 102nd Foot, faced a court martial at Chelsea for 'the act of Mutiny' in deposing him as Governor of New South Wales. A month later an unqualified verdict of guilty saw Johnston cashiered, though the only consequence was his retirement to his substantial farm in Australia. As a civilian Macarthur faced no charges in London but remained at legal risk in the colony until family lobbying persuaded the government to grant him indemnity from trial there eight years later. In the meantime he was, in effect, trapped in England while his able wife, Elizabeth, managed his Australian affairs with great success. This included pursuing his wool experiment using cross-bred merino sheep, though it only came to full fruition after Macarthur's return in 1817. As a result he still bears credit as one of the founders of the Australian wool industry, but he eventually died insane.

Bligh's promotion to rear-admiral, delayed until after the Johnston verdict, was confirmed in July 1811 and backdated a year. He did not serve again, except in advisory capacities, or long enjoy the company of his much-loved wife Betsy. She died in 1812 and was buried in their London parish churchyard of St Mary-at-Lambeth, leaving him with four unmarried daughters, one of whom was epileptic. (Harriet, the eldest child, married the wealthy panorama showman Henry Aston Barker in 1802.) He spent his last years at Farningham in Kent, rising by seniority to Vice-Admiral of the Blue before he died and his coffin joined Betsy's under an imposing monument at Lambeth. This still bears witness to him as 'the celebrated navigator who first transplanted the Bread fruit tree from Otaheite to the West Indies, bravely fought the battles of his country and died beloved, respected and lamented on the 7th day of December 1817, aged 64'. The church, however, now has a very different use: appropriately for a navigator whose fame – or notoriety – is forever linked to a botanical experiment, it is run by the Tradescant Trust as The Museum of Garden History.

The tomb of Bligh and his wife at the former church of St Mary's, Lambeth, London, overlooking the Thames beside Lambeth Palace.

CHAPTER FIVE

THE LOST VOYAGE OF ALEJANDRO MALASPINA

'For the past twenty years two nations, the English and the
French, in noble competition, have undertaken voyages of this
sort in which navigation, geography and humanity itself have
made very rapid progress … The proposed voyage would aim
to accomplish these objectives … But a voyage undertaken by
Spanish navigators must necessarily involve two other
objectives. One is the making of hydrographic charts covering
the most remote regions of America and the compilation of
sailing directions … The other is the investigation of the
political status of America both in relation to Spain and to
other European nations.'
– *Alejandro Malaspina, 'Plan for a Scientific and Political Voyage
Around the World', 10 September 1788*

The well-equipped expedition commanded by Alejandro Malaspina
which left Spain for the Pacific in 1789 represented at one level the
philosophical and scientific interests of European Enlightenment, at
another a determination to survey the Pacific rim of Spain's sprawling
overseas empire. It was intended to reassert the tradition of Spanish
voyaging in the *Mar del Sur* which had faded from view in the glare of
publicity that had accompanied the voyages of Cook, Bougainville and
Lapérouse. It would not be a voyage of discovery in the traditional sense,
Malaspina explained, for 'The safest and shortest routes between the most
distant corners of the earth had been pieced together. Any further voyage
of discovery would have invited scorn.'

No cost was spared in making the preparations. The corvettes
Descubierta ('discovery') and *Atrevida* ('audacious') were specially built for
the voyage, and carried the latest navigational and hydrographic
instruments. The officers, scientists and artists on board were carefully

80

Alejandro Malaspina. Painting by an unknown artist showing him dressed in the uniform of *Brigadier de la Real Armada* in 1795.

chosen by Malaspina, who had already completed one circumnavigation while on secondment to the Royal Philippines Company. Italian-born, he had joined the Spanish navy in 1774. He was an experienced hydrographic surveyor, having served, as had several of his officers, on Don Vicente Tofiño's comprehensive charting of the coasts of Spain. In addition, he was a man of wide reading and radical thinking, whose political and economic opinions were much influenced by Enlightenment scholars.

Unusually, the initiative for the voyage came from Malaspina and his fellow commander, José Bustamante, rather than from the Spanish government, and the expedition as a whole was seen by Malaspina as part of a global project of imperial regeneration. In the 'Plan for a Scientific and Political Voyage Around the World' which the two officers presented to the Spanish Navy Minister in September 1788, they emphasized that the scientific part of the voyage would follow the model of the expeditions of Cook and Lapérouse, as its members collected specimens and made hydrographic and astronomical observations. However, its political tasks would be directed towards strengthening Spain's national interests; for the expedition's duties would include making detailed charts of the coasts of Spanish overseas possessions, investigating the commercial and defensive capabilities of those territories and making political recommendations on their future. Furthermore, it would report on the Russian trading settlements rumoured to exist on the north-west coast of America and on the new British settlement just established at Botany Bay – 'places of interest whether from a commercial point of view or in the event of war'.

The voyage, Malaspina rather optimistically calculated, would take about three-and-a-half years. The expedition would enter the Pacific by way of Cape Horn, and sail along the coast from Chile to Mexico, across the North Pacific to the Sandwich Islands (Hawaii), then back to the American mainland to trace the coast north from California before visiting Canton. The second part of the voyage would take the corvettes to the Spanish possessions in Guam and the Philippines, south through the Indian Ocean to New Holland (Australia), and back into the Pacific to Tonga, the Society Islands and New Zealand, before returning home by the Cape of Good Hope to complete the circumnavigation. It was a hugely ambitious project and one whose political objectives of report, recommendation and reform marked it out from its British and French predecessors.

Surveys and investigations
The expedition sailed from Cadiz in July 1789, calling first at Montevideo, where the corvettes were overhauled after their maiden crossing of the Atlantic. The first year of the voyage along the Atlantic coast of Patagonia to the Falklands (Malvinas), round Cape Horn and along the Pacific coasts of Chile and Peru as far north as Callao, the port of the capital Lima, set the pattern for much of what was to follow. Along the coast running surveys were carried out and charts drawn. On land the officers busied themselves with triangulation surveys, the ships' chronometers were rated and a portable observatory was set up in order to make astronomical observations. Later in the voyage, when a specially designed pendulum arrived from Europe, observations for gravity were carried out in an attempt to determine the true shape of the Earth and, in particular, whether or not the northern hemisphere was flatter than the southern hemisphere (see p. 94). Meanwhile, at the various landing places the naturalists scoured the surrounding region for specimens, while the expedition's artists sketched people and places. This activity would have been familiar to Cook's men, but Malaspina's officers additionally spent much time questioning local officials and collecting information from the archives in pursuit of Malaspina's wider objective of reform of the overseas empire.

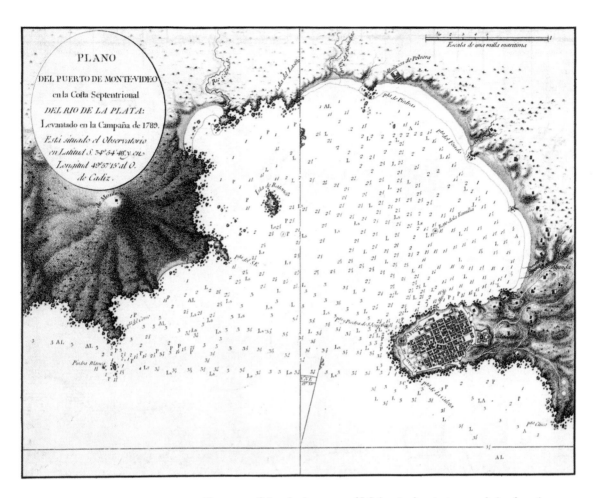

PLANO

DEL PUERTO DE MONTE-VIDEO

en la Cofta Septentrional

DEL RIO DE LA PLATA:

Levantado en la Campaña de 1789.

Eſtá ſituado el Obſervatorio

en Latitud S. 34°54'48' y en

Longitud 49°57'15' al O.

de Cadiz.

'Plano del Puerto de Monte-video'. Enqravinq based on Felipe Bauzá's survey of 1789. A fine example of the detailed hydrographic work carried out by the Malaspina expedition.

Because of the dual nature of Malaspina's mission, and the fact that the expedition was in Spanish waters for much of the voyage, it followed a rather different cycle of activity from that of its British and French predecessors in the Pacific. The corvettes spent about fifty per cent of their time in harbour and another ten per cent at anchor on coasts without harbour facilities. They were therefore at sea for only about forty per cent of the time, in contrast, for example, to the seventy per cent of the time that Cook's ships spent at sea on his second voyage. Although the stays in port allowed for plenty of fresh provisions, and scurvy was comparatively rare, time ashore was not an unmixed blessing, and Malaspina's journal is full of complaints about the problems presented by his crews once in port – ill-discipline, venereal disease and desertion. During the very first stay, at Montevideo, twenty-four men deserted, and the problem grew worse as the voyage proceeded. A table which Malaspina drew up at Acapulco in April 1791, twenty months or so into the voyage, showed that crew losses from one cause or another, but mostly from desertion, totalled 143 men. Given that the original complements of the corvettes were 102 men each, this was an extraordinarily high proportion.

The search for the Strait of Anian

Until its arrival at Acapulco, near the northern limits of Spanish settlement on America's west coast, the expedition had followed a predictable course, although the original timetable had slipped and Malaspina had decided that he would abandon the projected circumnavigation. Instead he aimed to return to Spain by the same route as his outward voyage, which would allow him to carry out more survey work in Chile and Patagonia. He now estimated that he would be away for five years. It was during the stay at Acapulco, as Malaspina prepared to sail across the Pacific to the Hawaiian Islands, that surprising, fresh instructions arrived from Spain. Malaspina was to head north to the Alaskan coast and search there for the passage to the Atlantic reportedly discovered by Lorenzo Ferrer Maldonado in 1588. For centuries the search for the North-West Passage had been encouraged by accounts of voyages that were supposed to have been made through the long-sought-after strait, but Ferrer Maldonado's story was the most extraordinary of them all. In 1609 he presented the Spanish court with a memorial in which he claimed that in 1588 he had made a voyage from Lisbon north through Davis Strait and well beyond the Arctic Circle, before sailing south-west for more than 2000 miles to latitude 60° north, where he reached the Pacific through the fabled Strait of Anian. This was the name given to the waterway thought to separate Asia and America, providing a navigable route between the Pacific and Atlantic oceans. According to Ferrer, the strait, whose zigzags he showed in several sketches, was fifteen leagues long with high, mountainous sides. Near its opening into the Pacific was a harbour capable of holding 500 ships, and while anchored there the Spanish ship encountered a large vessel bound for the Baltic with a rich cargo of pearls, gold, silks and porcelain. On the return voyage, the narrative continued, the Spaniards found temperatures in the Arctic warmer than those in the hottest parts of Spain.

The lack of interest in early seventeenth-century Spain in this farrago of nonsense is entirely understandable. What is more difficult to explain is why the 'discovery' should be have been taken seriously 200 years later, in a climate of opinion generally regarded as altogether more critical and less credulous, and after the failure of repeated attempts to find the North-West Passage. The French geographer Jean-Nicolas Buache de Neuville, who in 1790 presented the

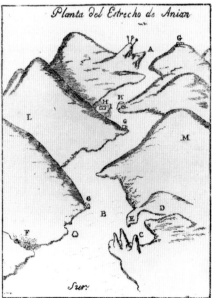

'Planta del Estrecho de Anian' is one of several views and maps with which Ferrer Maldonado accompanied his memorial of 1609. This view is taken from Carlo Amoretti, *Viaggio del Mare Atlantico al Pacifico per le Via del Nord-Ouest* (1811). The capital letters represent: A – north entrance of the strait; B – south entrance of the strait; C – port; D – river of pure water; E – place for a fort; F – canebrake; G – lookouts; H – bastions; L – part of Asia; and M – part of America.

prestigious Paris Academy of Sciences with a memoir supporting Ferrer Maldonado's account, must take much of the responsibility. Although the urgency of his new instructions must have startled Malaspina, he was familiar with the account, a copy of which had been found by one of his officers shortly before the expedition sailed. On several occasions in the first two years of the voyage Malaspina had referred to the account as being worth investigating, but by the time the expedition reached Acapulco he had decided to abandon the Alaskan stage of the voyage. The matter was now taken out of Malaspina's hands and he prepared to sail north. In an official response to Madrid he referred to some of the 'difficulties' in Ferrer's account, which in private letters he described as 'apocryphal' and 'false', while on the *Atrevida* Bustamante dismissed the account as fictitious and Buache's memoir as intended 'to delude Europe'. Bustamante pointed out that there was no resemblance between Ferrer Maldonado's description of the Alaskan coast and the recent surveys of Spanish and British vessels. In 1774 Juan Pérez had reached the Queen Charlotte Islands on the first Spanish expedition to the north-west coast, the next year Francisco de la Bodega y Quadra became the first Spaniard to land in Alaska, while in 1778 James Cook had sailed the length of the coast, although without making a close examination. These forays were followed by further Spanish voyages; by Ignacio de Arteaga in 1779 in a belated response to news of Cook's arrival on the coast, and then by Esteban José Martínez in 1788 and Salvador Fidalgo in 1790. Both Martínez and Fidalgo encountered Russian fur traders in Alaska, but neither they nor their predecessors on the coast came across what Ferrer Maldonado had described – a strait

Sketch by Felipe Bauzá of Malaspina's ships *Descubierta* and *Atrevida* at anchor off Mount St Elias, Alaska, in July 1791.

fifteen leagues long, a harbour large enough to hold 500 ships and vessels carrying Asian trade goods. It was in a mood of resignation rather than optimism, then, that Malaspina and Bustamante sailed north in May 1791, while a dozen seamen attempted to desert when they heard that their destination was Alaska, not Hawaii.

Malaspina took his ships on a long curving track well out to sea before heading in towards the Alaskan coast in latitude 56° north, near Cook's Cape Edgcumbe. The snow-covered mountains awed the journal keepers, and the cold was so intense that the artist Suria was unable to sketch on deck and was forced to retreat below to complete his drawings.

From this landfall the vessels sailed north towards the location of Ferrer Maldonado's supposed strait in latitude 60° north, and on 27 June were off Yakutat Bay. Despite earlier reservations, excitement grew on board as the *Descubierta* and *Atrevida* steered for a great cleft in the coastal range in latitude 59°15' north. Malaspina wrote that the inlet (Yakutat Bay) resembled that described by Ferrer Maldonado, and he added that 'imagination soon supplied a thousand reasons in support of hope'. Five years earlier the expedition of Lapérouse had approached Lituya Bay about a hundred miles to the south with similar hopes. Suria commented on the reaction of Malaspina's officers: 'They believed, and with some foundation, that this might be the so much desired and sought-for strait … Transported with joy our commander sailed towards the opening.' Even the sceptical Bustamante was caught up in the enthusiasm of the moment and entered in his journal that 'there was hardly anyone

José Cardero, 'Pira, y Sepulcros de la Familia del actual An-kau en el Puerto Mulgrave', 1791, showing members of the Malaspina expedition at the burial ground of a ruling Tlingit family at Port Mulgrave, Alaska.

among us who was not ready to believe in the probable existence of the longed-for passage'. By nightfall the corvettes had anchored inside the bay, close to a beach and a Tlingit village. Here the portable observatory was set up, the artists began sketching, wood and water were taken on board and a trade for sea-otter pelts took place.

By 2 July Malaspina was ready to explore in person the inner reaches of the inlet in search of the Strait of Anian. He took two launches and fifteen days' provisions and left Bustamante in charge of the ships. It took only a few hours to dispel all hopes, for soon the water shoaled and the thunderous sound of large chunks of ice calving from a glacier could be heard. Then the end of the inlet came in sight, its low shore blocked by a glacier behind which rose the steep walls of the coastal range. A frustrated Malaspina named the inlet Puerto del Desengaño (Disenchantment Bay), and after taking possession of the area headed out to sea. Much had been accomplished during the week's stay. The scientists on board had gathered

Alejandro Malaspina, 'Plano del Puerto del Desengaño'. This chart, printed in *Relación del Viaje hecho por las Goletas Sútil y Mexicana* (1802), shows Malaspina's survey by boat inside Yakutat Bay, Alaska, in July 1791. With his way blocked by the glacial ice shown here, Malaspina turned back and named the inlet 'Puerto del Desengaño' (Disenchantment Bay).

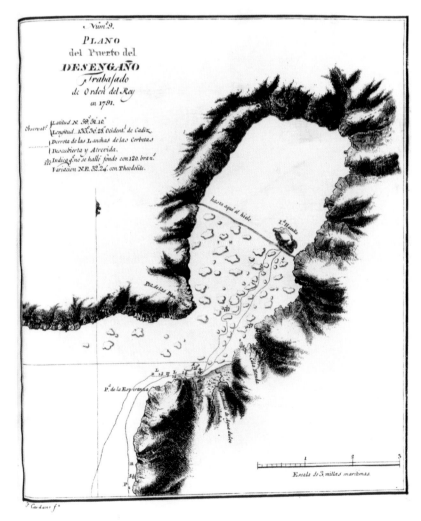

a rich harvest of ethnographic and natural history material, and the artists had made some superb sketches and paintings, but the overriding disappointment was that there was no strait leading deep into the interior. Later, Malaspina reflected in his journal that a reader in the twenty-first century would be amazed to see how seriously the fictitious accounts of Ferrer Maldonado and other navigators had been taken 'in an age which we call scientific and enlightened'.

From Alaska the ships sailed south to Nootka Sound, flashpoint of the diplomatic crisis of the previous year that had almost led to war between Spain and Britain, and then on to Monterey and Acapulco. On his arrival in Acapulco, Malaspina detached two of his officers, Dionisio Alcalá Galiano and Cayetano Valdés, to carry out a third and final season of Spanish explorations in the Strait of Juan de Fuca. They were instructed by Malaspina to give priority to inlets leading eastward 'to decide once and for all the excessively confused and complicated question of the communication or proximity of the Pacific Ocean and the Atlantic in this latitude'. In two small, locally built vessels, the *Sutil* and the *Mexicana*, Galiano and Valdés spent the summer of 1792 investigating the innermost recesses of the Strait of Juan de Fuca. While carrying out their survey the Spaniards encountered George Vancouver's Royal Navy ships, recently arrived on the coast and engaged on the same task. There was an exchange of information and mutual courtesies, but both sides continued with their independent surveys: the existence, or otherwise, of the North-West Passage was too politically sensitive an issue to be determined by the charts of foreign nationals. Painstaking work by Galiano and Valdés failed to reveal any way through to the east, although of openings, inlets and bays there were more than enough. By late August the Spanish vessels had sailed along the entire east or inner coast of Vancouver Island, and rounded its northern tip to gain the open ocean. On 31 August they arrived back at Nootka, having completed the first continuous circumnavigation by Europeans of Vancouver Island.

The Philippines, Port Jackson and Vava'u
By the end of 1791, as he prepared to set sail once more from Acapulco, Malaspina had finished the main part of his mission. His expedition had produced detailed charts of long stretches of the coasts of Spanish America, established the exact location of the main ports, carried out scientific experiments, collected vast numbers of natural history specimens (before the voyage ended just one of the naturalists had collected more than 15,000 plant specimens) and made observations and drawings of the native peoples from Patagonia to Alaska. Less openly, Malaspina had investigated the political and economic state of the colonies, with a view to drawing up recommendations for change. But in terms of distance and time the voyage was only half completed. There was the long run across the Pacific to the Philippines by way of Guam to be made before the ships turned south.

Malaspina spent almost nine months in the Philippines, while Bustamante in the *Atrevida* visited Macao on the coast of China to carry out gravitational observations. Malaspina's time in the Philippines was spent in making coastal surveys, while his naturalists headed off on inland excursions to collect specimens. During one of these trips the expedition's chief naturalist, the army officer Coronel Antonio Pineda, died – a heavy blow to Malaspina who wrote in his journal of the 'sudden and irreparable loss'. Malaspina's tribute to Pineda tells us much about his own views on the significance of the expedition's work:

> His ideas, as ambitious as they were viable, about the land and inhabitants of almost the entire continent of the Americas subject to the monarchy, the comparative exploitation of its minerals, the analysis of its languages, the administration, situation and customs of our colonies, although partially described in his notebooks, have largely perished with him.

After calling at Mindanao, south of the Philippines, the corvettes followed a semicircular track into the Pacific. They passed north of New Guinea and

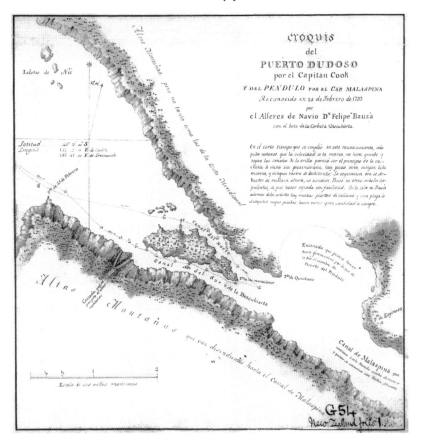

Felipe Bauzá, 'Croquis (sketch) del Puerto Dudoso'. Cook's Doubtful Sound was hurriedly surveyed by Bauzá in February 1793.

then east of the Solomon Islands, the New Hebrides (Vanuatu) and New Caledonia before sailing south to New Zealand. At the end of February 1793 Malaspina reached Cook's Doubtful Sound on the south-west coast of New Zealand's South Island, where he sent his cartographer Felipe Bauzá inshore in the pinnace to examine the area. Neither Cook nor any other European navigator had entered the sound, and Bauzá's chart for long remained the only survey of this stretch of water. On Bauzá's return Malaspina set an overnight course to Cook's Dusky Bay (today's Dusky Sound), but when bad weather made it too dangerous to enter he abandoned the attempt and sailed north-west to New South Wales and the newly established British convict settlement at Port Jackson.

Even before leaving Spain, Malaspina had suggested that New South Wales should be viewed for its political significance rather than as a region of interest to his naturalists. His month's stay at Port Jackson reflected this attitude. The courtesies exchanged by the Spanish officers and their British hosts no doubt reflected a genuine warmth between the two sides, but Malaspina's journal also revealed that the ceremonies enabled him to cast 'a veil over our national curiosity'. In effect, Malaspina was engaged in some discreet espionage in a colony which, he reported, had made astonishing progress in the five years since its founding. In a 'Political Examination of the English Colonies in the Pacific', Malaspina described the threat that the new colony posed to Spanish interests in the Pacific, possibly even serving as a base for an invasion of Chile and Peru in wartime. His answer to this danger was to suggest trading links between Spanish America and the colony by which cattle and provisions from

Fernando Brambila, 'Vista de la Colonia Inglesa de Sydney'. One of several views by Brambila showing the extent to which the colony at Port Jackson had developed since its establishment only five years before the visit of the Malaspina expedition in 1793 (see p. 35).

South America would find a profitable market in New South Wales and so turn a potential enemy into a satisfied trading partner. There was no realistic prospect that the Spanish government would adopt such a policy, but the recommendations reflected the unconstrained nature of Malaspina's thinking on economic and political matters.

On leaving Port Jackson Malaspina decided to sail directly to Vava'u, the northernmost group of islands in the Tongan archipelago. It had not been visited by Cook during his calls in Tonga during his second and third voyages, and Malaspina's stay there had an even clearer political purpose than that at Port Jackson. It was a follow-up to the visit made by the Spanish navigator Francisco Mourelle in 1781, and towards the end of his ten days at Vava'u Malaspina carried out only his second act of possession on the voyage. As at Yakutat Bay, site of the first act of possession, Vava'u had seen few European visitors, so the observations, descriptions and vocabularies compiled by Malaspina and his officers are of particular value. The sketches by the expedition's artists – in this instance Brambila and Ravenet – vividly supplement the written word. Relations with the islanders and their chief, Vuna, were friendly, apart from the inevitable incidence of petty thieving, and were characterized by the exchanges, commercial and sexual, that had become standard for European callers at the Pacific islands. All in all, the brief interlude at Vava'u had more in common with the previous voyages of the Cook era than any other part of the voyage, and Bustamante's remarks could have been taken from the pages of Hawkesworth or Bougainville:

Fernando Brambila, 'El Fondeadero de las Corvetas [*Descubierta* and *Atrevida*] en las Yslas de Vavao', a view of the anchorage at Vava'u in the Tonga Islands, May 1793. The observatory set up by the Spaniards is on the riqht.

> Nothing can compare to the beautiful variety of scenery that met our gaze on this little excursion. The regularity of the plantations, the graceful harmony of the landscape, and the confusion of evergreen trees scattered with flowers all spread before us the marvels of nature in

her brightest colours. In these delightful places the
dullest imagination could not resist the sweet and
peaceful sensations that they inspire. Here our minds
were gently drawn to philosophical reflections on the
life and happiness of these peoples … their tranquil
existence in the midst of abundance and pleasure.

Problems of discipline and health

The stay at Vava'u was marred by the unruly behaviour of the crew, many of
whom, Malaspina wrote, resented 'the restraint of discipline, however mild'.
This was now to be a recurrent theme. By this stage there were problems in
working the ships, for the crews were divided between worn-out sailors who
had been on board for the whole voyage and inexperienced youths from the
Philippines and elsewhere. Some indication of the strain Malaspina was
now under can be seen in an angry outburst in his journal, little more than
two weeks into the voyage from Vava'u across the Pacific to the South
American mainland. The trust that he had tried to build up with his crews
during the first part of the voyage had 'vanished like smoke'. More
worryingly, there was a breakdown in relations between Malaspina and his
officers, who were demanding 'more rest and fewer obligations'. The
situation was, he said, an odious one in which 'discipline was seen as
tyranny, caution as fear, and a normal desire for calm taken as a sign of
weakness'. He even hinted at the possibility of mutiny. The rift was also an
indication of Malaspina's own deterioration, certainly physically and perhaps
mentally and emotionally too. Not only had he been in command for almost
four years, but before sailing he had had only a few months of rest after his
circumnavigation in the service of the Royal Philippines Company.

When the corvettes reached Callao in Peru, Malaspina took his
instruments and books to the rural retreat of La Magdalena, away from
his squabbling officers. There, he wrote, he could 'shake off the hateful
guise of commanding officer and attend quietly to the restoration of my
own much weakened health'. His state of mind would not have been
helped by the fact that, unaccountably, he had not received any official
letters or instructions from Madrid since his second visit to Acapulco in
October 1791, more than two years earlier. He must have felt betrayed by
his closest associates and abandoned by his superiors.

Life ashore was disrupted by the news of the outbreak of war with
Revolutionary France, for this might have serious consequences for the
lightly armed corvettes. It accounts for Malaspina's decision that the
Descubierta and *Atrevida* should henceforth undertake separate passages to
Montevideo, both to increase the amount of surveying they could
undertake on the final part of the voyage and to reduce the risk of the
expedition and all its work being wiped out by a chance encounter with
enemy ships. So serious were the combined ravages of sickness and
desertion among the crews that Malaspina and Bustamante were able to
sail only after receiving fresh crew members from royal frigates already at

Callao. Of all Malaspina's problems the most intractable was the turnover of crew members. The records show that during the voyage about 215 served on board the *Descubierta* at different times, and about 240 on the *Atrevida*, making the total number of those who served on the two corvettes (each normally crewed by about a hundred men) in the region of 450. Fatalities among the 250 or so 'losses' suffered by the expedition seem to have been comparatively low at twenty named individuals, although undoubtedly there would have been further deaths among those crew members left behind in port hospitals whose fate is not known. What is certain is that Malaspina and his officers were faced with continual problems of training and discipline because of changes of crew, and his journal reflects his growing irritation with this situation.

With weakened crews, and worried by the prospect of meeting hostile ships, Malaspina dropped some of the more ambitious parts of the survey of the coasts of South America that he originally had in mind. He visited Port Egmont in West Falkand to carry out gravity observations and surveyed Puerto San Elena on the east coast of Patagonia, before making for Montevideo and his rendezvous with Bustamante. Off Cape Horn he set his own work, not for the first time, in the context of Cook's surveys:

> Once again we marvelled at the accuracy of Captain
> Cook's descriptions in this new scene of his navigational
> success and ability. Thus guided as if by his own hand,
> we put aside any ideas of discovery and assumed the
> equally useful role of correcting and at times improving,
> for public benefit and with a certain scientific curiosity,
> the original work, which will always be somewhat
> unfinished, however valuable and impressive ...

For his part Bustamante surveyed the Spanish settlement in Puerto de Soledad in East Falkland, and carried out a search for the Auroras Islands, reported to lie east of the Falklands, before rejoining Bustamante. The last stages of the voyage from Montevideo to Cadiz were an anticlimax as the *Descubierta* and the *Atrevida*, together with a royal frigate, escorted a convoy of slow-moving merchant ships across the potentially hostile waters of the Atlantic. Despite the frustrations of the crossing, Malaspina and his officers continued to make observations and to check their instruments, and it was wholly in character that the final sentence in Malaspina's last entry in his journal for 21 September 1794 concerned the rating of the chronometers. The expedition had been away for five years and two months.

Return and disgrace

On his return Malaspina busied himself in preparing the account of his voyage for publication. This would be an account on a grand scale that would dwarf the narratives of his predecessors in the Pacific, even the lavish three-volume account of Cook's last voyage. It would answer the accusation that Spain kept its discoveries secret. Rather, as Malaspina insisted, the publication of the results of his expedition would 'draw aside at last the thick curtain of mystery' which had concealed Spain's overseas possessions. In the first instance there would be seven volumes, an atlas of seventy charts, together with harbour plans and coastal views, and a folio of seventy drawings. Later, Malaspina hoped that there might be additional volumes of observations based on the work of the expedition's naturalists, Tadeo Haenke and Luis Neé. For Malaspina this monumental work would be more than a matter of factual record, for it would include, in his words, 'An assessment of the political state of the overseas empire, with detailed recommendations for change and reform'. In December 1794 he was received at court together with some of his officers but felt that he had been fobbed off with mere ceremony. His words in a letter to his friend Paolo Greppi show that deference and tact were not his strong points:

> One single day would have been sufficient to explain my
> system. I have seen everything, I have been everywhere.
> I had hoped that no matter the chaos of the present
> system it would be realised that there is but a small step
> from the wrong route to the right one, from absurdity to
> sane philosophy.

Nor did Malaspina confine himself to the state of the overseas empire, for at this time he presented the Navy Minister with a memoir setting out his views on the terms of a peace treaty with France. In commenting on so delicate a matter he enraged the powerful chief minister, Manuel Godoy, who referred to the memoir's 'lack of principles and moderation', and advised that Malaspina should burn it and be told to mend his ways.

Juan Ravenet, 'Experiencia del Pendulo Simple', gravity experiments by Malaspina (right-hand figure in the tent) and others at Port Egmont, West Falkland, in January 1794. This version has the artist, Ravenet, standing just outside the tent drawing the scene.

Malaspina was now treading on dangerous ground, although he was again received at court by the king and queen in March 1795 and was promoted to *brigadier* (admiral).

However, despite this sign of official favour, he became involved in clandestine political activities aimed at replacing Godoy and other ministers. In November, Malaspina was arrested, and after a hurried hearing of his case before the Council of State he was stripped of his rank and sentenced to ten years' imprisonment in the grim fortress prison of San Antón at La Coruña, while the officers who had been helping him to prepare his account of the voyage were ordered to stop work and to surrender all papers relating to the expedition.

Of the proposed seven-volume edition, only one volume was published, in 1802, and this dealt only with a subsidiary part of the expedition (the surveys carried out by Malaspina's officers, Galiano and Valdés, on detachment in the Strait of Juan de Fuca in 1792). The volume was an attempt to offset the publication of George Vancouver's account of his voyage, which included his rival survey of the Strait of Juan de Fuca, but although the Spanish account included a handsome atlas its appearance ten years after the event, and four years after the publication of Vancouver's narrative, was too little and too late. The volume contained no mention of Malaspina other than an occasional reference to the (unnamed) 'commander of the corvettes'. He had been removed from the historical record and so, for the most part, had his expedition, although its astronomical observations were published by one of his officers, José Espinosa y Tello in 1809. Oddly, the first appearance of Malaspina's own journal came in the form of a Russian translation, issued in parts in a naval periodical in St Petersburg in the 1820s after a Russian diplomat in Madrid obtained a copy of the Spanish original (which, less than ideally, was translated first into French and then into Russian). Finally, almost a hundred years after the expedition set sail an edited version of Malaspina's journal was published in Madrid in 1885, a belated attempt, as its editor said, at 'reparation'. After that the original journal in Malaspina's own hand had to wait until 1990 for publication in Spain as part of a multi-volume series devoted to the voyage. Only in the last fifteen years have the records of the expedition been published on the scale envisaged by Malaspina in 1794.

Malaspina was released from prison in 1803 but spent the remaining seven years of his life in exile in Italy. Although he seems to have had reasonable means during his retirement at Pontremoli (near his birthplace in Mulazzo), among the sad details of his last years is a document dated September 1806 recording that he had sold his sextant, that most personal and treasured of a sea officer's possessions. There was no rehabilitation, no restoration of his naval rank and no resumption of work on the ambitious edition of the voyage that he had planned so carefully. An expedition which had set new standards in terms of hydrographic, astronomical and natural history observations slipped from sight, and Alejandro Malaspina was for long the forgotten man among the Pacific navigators of the late eighteenth century.

CHAPTER SIX

'ACQUIRING A MORE COMPLETE KNOWLEDGE': GEORGE VANCOUVER IN THE NORTH PACIFIC

*J*ames Cook's chart of north-west America, made in the early summer of 1778 while he was hurrying north to begin his search for the North-West Passage in Alaska, was sketchy and inadequate. Pressed for time in foggy conditions, he had largely kept well offshore and his chart could do little more than indicate the general trends of the coast. While Cook showed that a navigable passage could not exist over the top of the American continent, it was theoretically possible after his voyage that one could still be found along the British Columbian coast. Thirteen years later, in 1791, the Admiralty ordered his old midshipman, George Vancouver, to finish the job and acquire for Britain 'a more complete knowledge' of this extraordinarily convoluted coastline which, with Cook's discovery of the rich trade in sea-otter furs, now had great commercial potential. Vancouver's finished chart reveals the size of the task that faced him: it took him three full seasons to chart an area that Cook had sailed along in four weeks, with most of the surveying having to be done from small open boats, often in appalling weather and with the political responsibility of resolving the Nootka Sound Crisis with the Spanish authorities (described in chapter one of this book) hanging over him. His survey stretched from California to Anchorage in Alaska and while it may have lacked the visionary sweep of Cook's great voyages, it was carried out with a determination, skill and an obsessive attention to detail that proved conclusively that no passage existed through the continent. It also resulted in a set of charts so accurate that many were still being used a hundred years later.

George Vancouver was born in King's Lynn, Norfolk, in 1757, the son of the deputy collector of customs, and at the age of fourteen he was entered on the *Resolution*'s books as an able seaman for Cook's second

George Vancouver (1757–98). Oil painting by an unknown artist. The identification of Vancouver in this painting has been disputed.

voyage. He was really one of the ship's 'young gentlemen', trainee officers destined for commissions once they had served the required period at sea and passed the lieutenant's examination. He did his job well, if unspectacularly, a fellow young gentleman describing him as 'a Quiet inoffensive Young man'. In later life Vancouver claimed to have sailed nearer the South Pole than anyone else on this voyage, for when Cook decided that at 71°10' south he had pushed as far as was humanly possible Vancouver scrambled out on to the bowsprit, waved his hat over his head and shouted '*ne plus ultra*' – nothing further. The only source of this story is Vancouver himself and if true it has a certain irony, for, as one of his officers later remarked, he 'was never known to put a favourable construction on the follies of youth'. However, he was a capable officer and for Cook's third voyage he was appointed midshipman in Captain Clerke's *Discovery*.

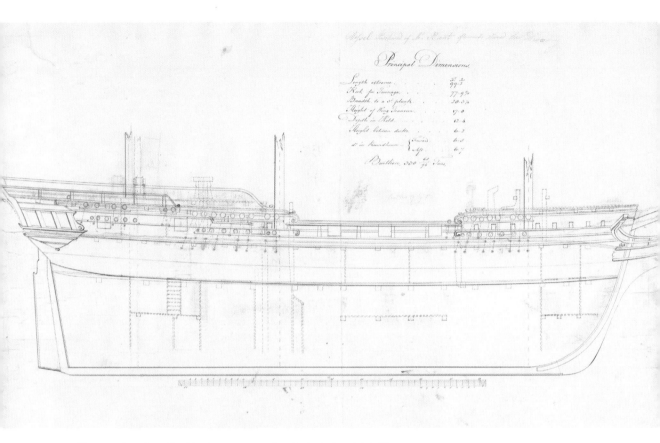

Principal Dimensions

Admiralty plan of *Discovery*, as bought from Randall and Brent, Deptford. The major alterations needed to turn the merchant ship into a sloop for exploration are shown in green.

Two weeks after Cook's ships returned to Britain in 1780, Vancouver passed his lieutenant's examination and was appointed to a sloop under orders for the West Indies. With the exception of a sixteen-month period on half-pay, he spent the next seven years in the Caribbean, rising to be first lieutenant of the 50-gun *Europa* and recommending himself to the commander-in-chief of the West Indies Station, Commodore Sir Alan Gardner, by surveying Jamaica's Kingston Harbour. The survey was completed with the assistance of the *Europa*'s master, Joseph Whidbey, and the charts themselves were drawn by Joseph Baker, one of the midshipmen, beginning a professional association between the three men that would flower on the north-west coast of America.

The ship selected for Vancouver's voyage was named after Cook's *Discovery* of 1776–80. She was a merchantman converted for exploration which had been lying for more than a year in the River Thames under the command of another of Cook's old officers, Henry Roberts, waiting for orders to survey the Southern Whale Fisheries, a large area encompassing the southern Pacific and Atlantic oceans. Vancouver received an appointment as *Discovery*'s first lieutenant in 1790, almost certainly through the influence of Gardner, who had just become one of the Lords of the Admiralty. During the Spanish Armament of 1790 – Britain's military response to the Nootka Sound Crisis – the fleet was put on a war

Watercolour of the *Discovery* being fitted out at Deptford. This was acquired by the National Maritime Museum in 2005 and is the only known original drawing of *Discovery* as an exploration vessel other than the Admiralty plan (opposite).

footing. *Discovery*'s crew was redistributed and the planned voyage of exploration suspended. Once a political solution was agreed with Spain, however, the ship was given new orders which combined taking formal possession of the disputed land at Nootka Sound with a survey of the north-west coast on which, under the terms of the new agreement, Britain now had the right to trade. For reasons which are no longer clear, Roberts was relieved of his command and Vancouver appointed in his place.

Sir Joseph Banks had been closely involved in planning Roberts' voyage but there was immediate friction between him and Vancouver. Banks had persuaded the Admiralty to build a 12- x 8-foot 'plant cabbin' on the quarterdeck to house the collection of live plants he hoped would be brought back, and he personally supervised its installation at Deptford; but Vancouver loathed the large, heavy structure that intruded on the limited deck space and made the ship difficult to handle. Banks had also appointed a Scottish naval surgeon named Archibald Menzies to make 'an investigation of the whole of Natural History of the Countries you are to visit; as well as an enquiry into the present state and comparative degree of civilization of the inhabitants you meet with'. Menzies was an excellent choice for he was a talented naturalist who already knew the area, having just returned from James Colnett's fur-trading voyage to the North Pacific; but he was unambiguously Banks's man. He was appointed to Vancouver's ship as a supernumerary botanist, not as a naval surgeon, and this position placed him outside the ship's formal chain of command, giving him a privileged and protected status that Vancouver was clearly uneasy about – as well as a salary of £150 a year which, an irritated

Vancouver later pointed out to the Admiralty, was double his own pay. For his own part, Banks was used to being treated with deference by naval officers and was annoyed by Vancouver's 'arrogance':

> How Captain Vancouver will behave to you [Menzies] is more than I can guess, unless I was to judge by his conduct toward me – which was such as I am not used to receive from one in his station ... As it would be highly imprudent in him to throw any obstacle in the way of your duty, I trust he will have too much good sense to obstruct it.

Banks advised Menzies to make a note when he felt Vancouver was being obstructive, which he dutifully did. Vancouver had a much freer hand in selecting his officers, however. Joseph Whidbey was appointed *Discovery*'s master, another shipmate from *Europa*, Peter Puget, became his second lieutenant, while his third was Joseph Baker. The first lieutenant, Zachary Mudge, had also served briefly on the *Europa*, although he almost certainly got the job through his connections to the powerful Pitt family. *Discovery* was to be accompanied by the brig *Chatham*, commanded by Lieutenant William Broughton. A storeship, *Daedalus*, commanded by Richard Hergist, another of Cook's old officers and one of Vancouver's ex-messmates on the old *Discovery*, was to sail to the Pacific separately and rendezvous with them at either Hawaii or Nootka Sound.

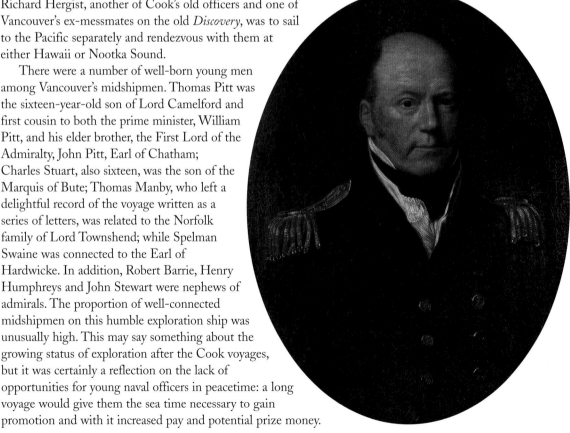

William Broughton (1762–1821), by an unidentified artist. Commander of the *Chatham*, he is painted here as a captain in later life.

There were a number of well-born young men among Vancouver's midshipmen. Thomas Pitt was the sixteen-year-old son of Lord Camelford and first cousin to both the prime minister, William Pitt, and his elder brother, the First Lord of the Admiralty, John Pitt, Earl of Chatham; Charles Stuart, also sixteen, was the son of the Marquis of Bute; Thomas Manby, who left a delightful record of the voyage written as a series of letters, was related to the Norfolk family of Lord Townshend; while Spelman Swaine was connected to the Earl of Hardwicke. In addition, Robert Barrie, Henry Humphreys and John Stewart were nephews of admirals. The proportion of well-connected midshipmen on this humble exploration ship was unusually high. This may say something about the growing status of exploration after the Cook voyages, but it was certainly a reflection on the lack of opportunities for young naval officers in peacetime: a long voyage would give them the sea time necessary to gain promotion and with it increased pay and potential prize money.

Discovery and *Chatham* left Plymouth on the unpropitious date of 1 April 1791, entering the Pacific via Cape Town, south Australia and New Zealand. On the way south there was an incident in Tenerife in which Vancouver was accidentally pushed into the harbour while trying to stop a brawl between drunken members of his crew and a Spanish shore patrol. Menzies described it in detail to Banks and was of the opinion that 'the quarrel originated with our people'. It was probably started by Midshipman Pitt who, in a rare moment of good sense, promptly escaped by jumping into the sea. Vancouver never informed the Admiralty of this embarrassing incident, which was unfortunate as Banks made sure it became widely known.

Chart of Dusky Bay, New Zealand, after James Cook; from George Vancouver's *A Voyage of Discovery to the North Pacific Ocean and Round the World* (1798).

At the beginning of November 1791, the two ships reached Dusky Bay (now Dusky Sound), New Zealand, a harbour favoured by Cook. Cook had already surveyed the bay, producing a chart that Thomas Manby thought had a 'degree of accuracy and exactness' that would forever 'stand a monument of his unremitted diligence and a conspicuous

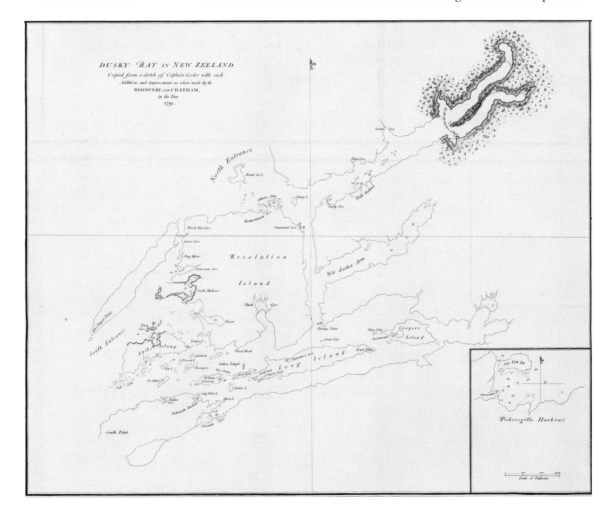

testimony of his unwearied assiduity'. But Cook had left two small branches at the head of Dusky Bay unexplored, noting on the chart 'No Body Knows What'; Vancouver surveyed them and in great good humour changed the name to 'Some Body Knows What'. The two ships then set off across the Pacific for Tahiti where, wrote Manby in a mood of eager anticipation, 'the men are benevolent and friendly; the women generous and beautiful'. They arrived on 29 December 1791. In fact, *Chatham* had arrived a few days earlier: it was already becoming a bit of a joke – an irritating one to the crew of the *Discovery* – that when the two ships sailed together *Chatham*'s slow sailing held them up, but as soon as they sailed separately *Chatham* would always beat the senior ship.

After the mutiny on the *Bounty* in 1789, it would be many years before Royal Navy captains would enter Polynesia without being at least aware of the potentially destabilizing charms of the islanders. Vancouver, therefore, issued strict orders to manage trade and keep the crew and the young gentlemen on board unless they were required to go ashore on duty. His orders tried to control contact rather than stop it but they were none the less deeply resented: George Hewitt, the surgeon's mate, suggested acidly that when Vancouver had last been in Tahiti in 1777 he had been 'a Young Man, but that not being now the case the Ladies were not so attractive' to him. Midshipman Pitt was flogged for trying to exchange a piece of iron barrel-hoop for sex, guilty in Vancouver's eyes of disobedience, illegal trade and the misuse of ship's equipment. Flogging such a well-connected young man was not a good career move for Vancouver and (since warrant officers were supposedly exempt) neither did it receive universal approbation on the ship. Pitt had a dangerously unstable personality but he was also a powerful character who would have considerable influence once he inherited his father's title. He also clearly had a following on *Discovery*, particularly among the midshipmen. Shortly after leaving Tahiti a drunken Midshipman Stuart pulled a razor from his pocket, brandished it in front of his captain and proclaimed, 'If, Sir, you ever flog me, I will not survive the disgrace: I have this ready to cut my throat with.' The issue, to these well-born young men, was one of 'honour' and it was destined to become a recurrent theme on Vancouver's quarterdeck.

Vancouver's relations with the rulers of Tahiti and the Hawaiian Islands were, by contrast, generally assured and astute. In Hawaii, where his ships would return to winter in 1792–93 and 1793–94, he took pains to be friendly and diplomatic, even though as a witness of Cook's death he was understandably cautious. Over the course of his three visits to the islands it became clear that Vancouver saw their strategic importance to the development of trade in the North Pacific more clearly than most. Hawaii had gained a deserved reputation as a dangerous place for lightly armed and lightly manned merchant ships and, although it was nowhere in his orders, Vancouver understood part of his mission as being to make the islands safer for European shipping. Establishing a good working relationship with Kamehameha and Kahekili, the two pre-eminent and warring rulers of the island group, was the starting point for this strategy, which, it later emerged, formed part of Vancouver's larger ambition to annexe Hawaii. Later in the voyage he took formal possession of a part of the North American coast, in what is now Oregon, also without orders, which suggests that from the first he saw his voyage as counterpart to the settlement of New South Wales and part of an active British development of the whole Pacific region.

Vancouver's behaviour could be unpredictable, however. Furious about the theft of some linen in Tahiti, he put a noose round the neck of a Tahitian he knew was merely an accomplice and, according to the ever-critical George Hewitt, 'in a Passion snatched hold of the Halter himself and drew it so tight as nearly to deprive the Man of Life…'. In Maui (one of the Hawaiian Islands) the following winter a few ribbons were stolen and Vancouver 'put himself in such a passion and threatened the chiefs with such menacing threats' that the chief of the island hurriedly leapt out of a window and into his canoe. Vancouver was intolerant of theft and this trait would later be interpreted by his detractors as an obsession with property which supposedly revealed that, while he may have been an officer, he was certainly no gentleman.

Vancouver was to start his survey in the Strait of Juan de Fuca, named after a Greek pilot in the service of Spain who was supposed to have sailed up the Californian coast in the 1590s and into a large inlet, the entrance to which was marked by 'a great Hedland or Island, with an exceedingly high Pinnacle or spired Rocke, like a pillar thereupon'. De Fuca claimed to have followed its course for some twenty days before reaching the Atlantic and 'discovering' the North-West Passage. Cook passed by in 1778: 'It is in the very latitude we were now in where geographers have placed the pretended *Strait of Juan de Fuca*, but we saw nothing like it, nor is there the least probability that iver any such thing exhisted.'

But strait there was and one that was indeed marked by a pinnacle of rock, today called Fuca Pillar. Vancouver's ships entered cautiously in 'very thick rainy weather' in April 1792, sailing along the south coast of the strait, which he called the 'Continental Shore'. His plan was simplicity itself: he would keep this shore on his right hand knowing that whatever its twists, turns and blind alleys he would either feel his way into the North-West Passage or find himself back in the open ocean. The next morning dawned with 'clear and pleasant weather', wrote Vancouver, although Manby's prose was more poetic:

> Never was contrast greater, in this days sailing than with
> that we had long been accustomed too. It had more the
> aspect of enchantment than reality, with silent admiration
> each discerned the beauties of Nature, and nought was
> heard on board but expressions of delight murmured from
> every tongue. Imperceptibly our Bark skimmed over the
> glassy surface of the deep, about three Miles an hour, a gentle
> breeze swelled the lofty Canvass whilst all was calm below.

The idyll was cruelly dashed for Manby when he joined his captain in a search for an anchorage, landed and 'killed a remarkable animal about the size of a cat, of a brown color, with a large, white, bushy tail that spread over his back. After firing I approached him and was saluted by a discharge from him the most nauseous and fetid my sense of smelling ever experienced'. Archibald Menzies was keen to take it on board for examination and tied the body to the bow of the cutter, but the smell 'was so intolerable' that it was thrown in the water. The skunk's revenge could never be entirely eradicated from Manby's clothes despite numerous soakings in boiling water and a chastened midshipman vowed never to disturb another 'on any consideration'.

The two ships anchored in a large bay, which Vancouver named Port Discovery, where three of the ships' boats were victualled for a week and the survey began. As they started, the weather changed and the gentle breeze that had so enraptured Manby gave way to gales and fog. Obedient to Vancouver's plan to follow the continental shore, over the next few weeks the boats began to trace the coast south into Puget Sound, following every waterway until it either returned them to their starting point or ceased to be navigable. They employed an enhanced version of the 'running survey' that had been used to such good effect by Cook, landing frequently to establish their positions by astronomical observation and measuring base lines on the beach to ensure that their triangulations were accurate. Vancouver soon 'became thoroughly convinced that our boats alone could enable us to acquire correct or satisfactory information regarding this broken country' although he admitted with masterly understatement that 'the execution of such a service in open boats would necessarily be extremely laborious'. Menzies' description of one night during the first survey was typical of many: his boat was battling against a strong ebb tide 'and the night was so very dark & foggy with excessive rain' that they gave up the hope of finding the prearranged rendezvous and pulled ashore to pitch their tents and kindle a fire, but 'the latter was found a very difficult task it being so dark & every thing so wet, it was midnight before we could get under any kind of shelter & then every thing about us was completely drenched & in this situation the greatest part of the Boats Crews passed the night without any covering to shelter them from the inclemency of the weather'. The survey would henceforth be carried out almost exclusively in the boats, rowed mile after aching mile, with the surveyors completing their observations in sections that were then added to the master chart being drawn up by Joseph Baker on *Discovery* and *Chatham*. The ships would then weigh anchor, move further up the coast, anchor again, and the boats would set out once more.

As the survey progressed over the next three seasons, Vancouver would sight, plot and name hundreds of headlands, bays, mountains and islands. Some complimented old shipmates such as the astronomer, William Wales, who taught Vancouver the principles of navigation and surveying on Cook's second voyage and who was remembered in Wales Point.

Chart of the area around Vancouver Island surveyed in 1792; from Vancouver's *A Voyage of Discovery*.

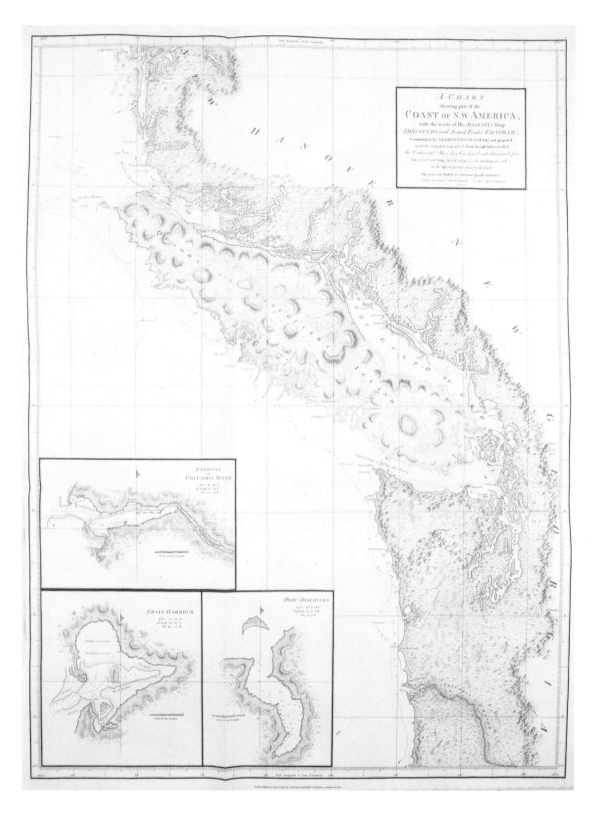

Others honoured royalty or Admiralty officials – King George Sound and Cape Chatham, for example – or influential people – Port Townshend, named, as Thomas Manby put it, 'in honor of the noble marquis, my sincere and long known friend'. Countless names were descriptive: Desolation Sound is now considered a beauty spot but Vancouver thought it 'a gloomy place' and one that 'afforded not a single prospect that was pleasing to the eye'. A crewman died after eating bad mussels at Poison Cove and New Dungeness was so called because Vancouver thought it bore a strong resemblance to Dungeness in Kent. He finished his survey three long years later at Port Conclusion.

Vancouver's charts inscribed a specifically British nomenclature on the landscape, reflecting and reinforcing Britain's emerging ambitions in the area but obscuring a story of contact with Native Americans. A significant side-effect of Vancouver's decision to survey from small boats was the constant, if brief, encounters with the many different peoples living along the coast. In the first survey from Port Discovery alone they passed through the territories of five different clans, and would eventually come into contact with all of the six major language groups on the north-west coast: Wakashan, Haida, Tsimshian, Tlingit, Eyak-Athapaskan and, far to the north, the Chugach. The study of people was hampered by the lack of a professional artist like Hodges or Webber, and, while Vancouver's officers made competent sketches of places and incidents, they were surveyors and their drawings were primarily topographical, with human figures almost entirely absent. Some of the published engravings did include people but they were the later additions of the artist, William Alexander, who was hired after the voyage to improve the sketches for publication, and they have no ethnographic value. Menzies had official responsibility for ethnography and he steadily collected Native artefacts while the descriptions of peoples left by him, Vancouver and some other

K3, by Larcum Kendall, London, 1774. The chronometer that accompanied both Vancouver and Flinders on their voyages.

'Four remarkable supported Poles in Port Townsend, Gulph of Georgia'; by John Sykes, but 'improved' by William Alexander, in Vancouver's *A Voyage of Discovery*. Some sixty-five drawings survived from the voyage, mainly by midshipmen Sykes and Humphrys, some of which were later engraved to illustrate Vancouver's published journal. This engraving shows the high poles found in several Native American villages and which puzzled Vancouver's men. The poles were actually used to suspend nets to trap birds.

'Exploring an island' by John Sykes, as improved by William Alexander; from Vancouver's *A Voyage of Discovery*.

officers are valuable source material for scholars to this day. But although not an unsympathetic observer, and admittedly hampered by the briefness of the meetings, Menzies was never really as curious about human beings, their origins and cultures as J. R. Forster had been on Cook's second voyage, and his ethnography does not compare to that of his predecessor.

Menzies began his botanical collections in Port Discovery with the first specimens of the oriental strawberry tree, the arbutus which bears his name, *Arbutus menziesii*. This, he wrote, 'grows to a small tree & was at this time a peculiar ornament to the Forest by its large clusters of whitish flowers & ever green leaves, but its peculiar smooth bark of a reddish brown colour will at all times attract the Notice of the most superficial observer'. Here, too, he collected the *Rhododendron macrophyllum*, later adopted as the state of Washington's flower. Menzies' most famous introduction to the gardens of Europe was the monkey-puzzle tree, *Araucaria araucana*, which he obtained not in North America but from nuts collected in Chile on the way home. They were planted at Kew and one, which was known as 'Sir Joseph Banks's Pine', was sketched in the 1830s and is thought to have survived until the end of the nineteenth century.

Menzies put his live specimens in Vancouver's hated 'plant cabbin' but keeping them alive was a constant struggle. 'I have not yet been able to get plants to succeed,' he complained to Banks: 'to my mind in the Frame on the Quarter Deck – for if it is uncovered in rainy weather to admit air, the dripping from the rigging impregnated with Tar & Turpentine hurts the foliage & soil – and if the Side lights are opened Goats – Dogs – Cats – Pigeons – Poultry &c. &c. are ever creeping in & destroying the plants.' He lost an entire collection almost overnight in the cold Alaskan spring, and many more in a sudden squall when homeward bound in the Atlantic.

The survey seemed an endless task at times and tempers became frayed. Menzies and Vancouver clashed over the plant frame and were soon communicating only in writing on the subject. The capable Manby got a brutal dressing down from Vancouver for losing touch with the lead boat one night: 'His salutation I can never forget', wrote the deeply offended midshipman, 'and his language I will never forgive unless he withdraws his words by a satisfactory apology.' Vancouver may have been quick-tempered and abusive but he still recognized talent and steadily promoted Manby during the voyage, appointing him master of the *Chatham*; 'a situation I should have refused in England', Manby said, but welcomed in America 'as it cleared me from a man I had just reason to be displeased with'. Despite his promotions, Manby was true to his word and never did forgive Vancouver. Neither did Midshipman Pitt, who was punished twice more in the first surveying season, being beaten for breaking the glass of the binnacle in a piece of horseplay and put in irons for falling asleep on watch. Vancouver was equally hard with his crew, on one occasion making them tack the ship all day – an exhausting procedure – when he felt that they had been too slow on the first tack.

Arbutus Menziesii, the strawberry tree or Pacific Madrone, found by Archibald Menzies at Port Townsend. A nineteenth-century lithograph.

And so the first summer progressed, the two ships painstakingly charting the continental shore between the future sites of Seattle and Vancouver. It was near the latter that they met two small Spanish survey vessels, the *Sutil* and *Mexicana*, offshoots of the Malaspina expedition. They were able to tell Vancouver that Don Francisco de la Bodega y Quadra was already waiting in Nootka Sound as agreed by the Spanish and British governments for the final resolution of the 'incident'. Meanwhile, Vancouver and the commanders of *Sutil* and *Mexicana* agreed to pool the results of their surveys, Vancouver honourably recording Spanish names on his charts where they had been the first to survey a coast. Most of the Spanish names, however, were excised and Vancouver's names restored when the charts were prepared for publication back in Britain.

The four ships eventually separated and *Discovery* and *Chatham* wriggled through a long and narrow passage that after a hundred miles opened out into the broad waters of Queen Charlotte Sound to the north of Vancouver Island. The maze of shoals they found here was far more dangerous than the narrows and *Discovery* soon ran aground on a falling tide. Vancouver quickly lightened the ship and ordered the topmasts and yards to be brought down so their weight would not drag the ship over. However, despite these precautions, Manby recorded that 'after lying upright for half an hour a terrible crash ensued which brought the ship on her broadside'. In bad conditions *Discovery* could have been lost but fortunately it was calm and the ship floated off with the rising tide some hours later. They had no sooner got off and rerigged than *Chatham* ran aground and an exasperated Vancouver eventually had to send the boats ahead to find a safe passage.

It was now getting towards the end of August and Vancouver turned his ships towards Nootka Sound to begin negotiations with Bodega y Quadra and rendezvous with the storeship, *Daedalus*, which was waiting for them, but with sad news: Vancouver's old friend Richard Hergist and the young astronomer, William Gooch, whose appointment had arrived too late for him to sail on the *Discovery*, had been killed in a brief and

'The *Discovery* on the Rocks in Queen Charlotte's Sound', by Zachary Mudge, as improved by William Alexander; from Vancouver's *A Voyage of Discovery*.

confused affray on one of the Hawaiian Islands.

Vancouver's negotiations with Bodega y Quadra were amicable – a mark of their mutual respect was their naming of Quadra and Vancouver Island, which only later became Vancouver Island – but they could not reach agreement on the restitution of British property in the sound and a frustrated Vancouver wrote to the Admiralty for further instructions (which were never given him). He then headed south to Monterey where official reports, charts and specimens were sent back to Britain, while others took the opportunity to send letters home:

> We are my good fellow [wrote Manby] spinning about the
> Globe like a Worligig, seldom in a place, and as seldom like
> true Seamen contented with our situation. Good health
> continues in our little squadron, though I am sorry to add
> not that good fellowship which ought to subsist with
> adventurers traversing these distant seas, owing to the
> conduct of our Commander in Chief who is grown
> Haughty Proud Mean and Insolent, which has kept himself
> and his Officers in a continual state of wrangling …

Leaving Monterey, they sailed for the Hawaiian Islands to overwinter.
While there Vancouver made strenuous efforts to bring Hergist's and
Gooch's killers to justice and, with the help of the Hawaiian rulers, tried
and executed three men off Oahu's Waikiki beach. Hewitt, inevitably,
criticized the procedure suggesting that there was no evidence that any of
the men had been involved in the killing, but his sentiments do not appear
to have been shared by the rest of the crew and even Manby approved.
The Hawaiian chiefs, vying for political control among themselves, cooperated because their powerful visitor was a useful ally.

Vancouver returned to Nootka Sound in the spring, beginning the
survey where they had finished the previous autumn, and the ships
gradually worked their way north along an even more intricate coastline.
Vancouver had been a sick man before the voyage even started, probably
having contracted some form of glandular disease during his time in the
West Indies, but by the second surveying season his health was worsening
and he was unable to take personal command of as many of the survey
trips as before. However, he had made sure during the winter that the
boats' crews now had covers to protect them from the incessant rain, bags
for dry clothes and lockers in which to store provisions. The weather was
appalling and the Natives, he wrote, seemed 'more daring and insolent'
than those in the area around Vancouver Island. They were now in the
territory of the Tlingit and that August Vancouver recorded 'an
unprovoked attack on our boats' during which several Natives were killed.
His boat had landed to fix the outline of the shore and, although four or
five Tlingit canoes also landed close by, Vancouver was unconcerned as
they appeared 'peaceably inclined' and eager to trade at first. Then the
Tlingit began stealing objects and seemed increasingly 'inclined to be
turbulent'. 'Our situation', Vancouver wrote, 'was now become very critical
and alarming'; one of the crew was stabbed in the thigh and he abandoned
his policy of avoiding bloodshed and opened fire, killing between six and
twelve people – the British estimates varied widely – before being able to
pull away to the safety of his accompanying boats.

Vancouver was unsure whether in landing he had unwittingly
committed an offence, or if the attack had been in revenge for 'injuries
they have sustained from other civilized visitors', by which he meant fur
traders, or if the situation had escalated when 'they conceived the valuable

articles we possessed'. In this case the probability is that the motive was avarice but any one of the theories could have been valid. Encounters between Natives and British, neither of whom understood the other's taboos, cultures or languages, were always complex and potentially fraught affairs, especially as Vancouver's boats were conducting their surveys close inshore and landing often. The British frequently complained of Native thefts, for example, but helped themselves freely to wood, water, game and greenstuff, little comprehending that these things had owners and needed to be paid for, while Menzies' interest in burial sites and Native bones involved trespassing on sacred ground. The violence in what Vancouver referred to as 'Traitor's Cove' was one of the very few occasions on which blood was spilt, which, bearing in mind the tensions inherent in the meetings, shows remarkable forbearance on both sides. The majority of meetings were peaceful and trading often brisk – too brisk, according to Thomas Manby, who in a letter to a friend accused his captain of using government trade goods to buy sea-otter furs on his own account, so 'pursuing business and a Trade … unbecoming the Character of an officer in his Honorable and exalted station'.

At some point during this season Midshipman Pitt transgressed for the last time and an unknown member of the crew left a fragmentary record of his illegal trade and punishment:

> the Capt. missing some sheets of copper cd not learn who had taken them he therefore tied up the Boatswain … during the flogging the Boatswain feeling the pain said Oh Mr. Pitt how can you see me thus used. Capt. V. perceiving that Mr. Pitt had taken the copper ordered the boatswain to be released and Mr. P. to take as many lashes as the boatswain had recd.

Vancouver had had enough of Pitt and when the ship returned to Hawaii the following winter he sent him and a couple of other troublemakers back home. During the winter of 1793–94 Vancouver had a diplomatic victory on Hawaii when 'the principal chiefs of the island … unanimously ceded the said island of Owyhee to His Britannic Majesty, and acknowledged themselves to be subjects of Great Britain'. Vancouver overstated his case as Kamehameha was only putting Hawaii under the protection of Britain, and had his own purposes, but it was a skilful piece of diplomacy none the less and one that would have secured an important strategic base for Britain had the fur trade developed. Curiously, Vancouver never informed the Admiralty and the first the British government appears to have heard of the cession of Hawaii was when Vancouver's journal was published in 1798, by which time he was dead.

The following spring the ships returned to North America and this time Vancouver sailed straight to Cook's River, the northern extremity of the survey. Sixteen years earlier, it had seemed to Cook's officers to hold promise of being the North-West Passage they sought, but Cook cut short the survey, writing tetchily in his journal that they had all wasted enough time on a 'triffling point of geography'. Vancouver briskly established that no navigable 'river' existed and changed the name to Cook's Inlet, noting in his journal that 'had the great and first discoverer of it, whose name it bears, dedicated one more day to its further examination, he would have spared the theoretical navigators, who have followed him in their closets, the task of ingeniously ascribing to this arm of the ocean a channel, through which a north-west passage … might ultimately be discovered'. It would have saved Vancouver much trouble as well, but this remains unsaid in a rare criticism of the captain he normally revered.

The two ships steadily worked south, finishing at the end of August 1794 at 56° north, Port Conclusion, where the north-going survey had ended the previous year. When the boats finally returned after their last extended survey, Vancouver proudly wrote:

> the hearty congratulations that were mutually exchanged by
> three cheers, proclaimed not only the pleasure that was felt
> in the accomplishment of this laborious service, but the zeal
> with which it had been carried into execution, and …
> laudable pride … in having been instrumental to the
> attainment of so grand an object.

There was also a strong sense of relief: Midshipman Barrie probably spoke for many when he said that he would never go through another such voyage 'if a Post Captain's commission was to be my reward'. It had been a hard, troubled but successful expedition. The boats had charted more than 5000 miles of heavily indented and dangerous coastline with, Vancouver said, 'a degree of minuteness far exceeding the letter of [his] commission'. He had lost but six men and only one of them to disease. Although himself a very sick man and with nagging concerns that he had never managed to resolve the Nootka Sound problem, he was clearly looking forward to a happy return and the recognition he felt he deserved. It was not to be, however, for the waters in London were to prove far more treacherous than those of America.

In the intervening years Sir Joseph Banks had been busy maliciously planting the shipboard gossip sent back by Menzies along with his regular packages of seeds. Banks got more useable information when he heard that the simmering feud over the plant frame had erupted one last and violent time on the way home, and that Vancouver had placed the naturalist under arrest and had demanded a court martial as soon as they landed. The affair was smoothed over when Menzies apologized to Vancouver, who then dropped charges. Banks, however, continued his campaign, encouraging Menzies to publish an account of the voyage before Vancouver's official narrative; but, Menzies being 'but a slow hand with the pen', the book never materialized.

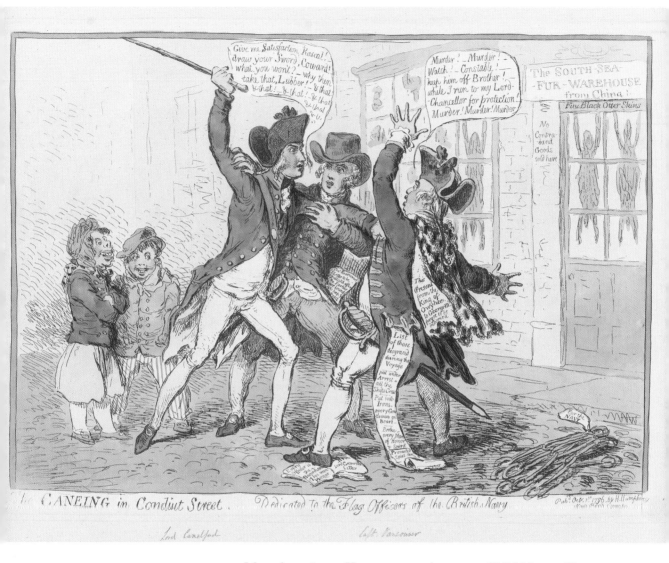

'The Caneing in Conduit Street', coloured etching by James Gillray, 1796. This satirical cartoon shows the infamous incident in September that year when Thomas Pitt, by now Lord Camelford, tried to give George Vancouver a public thrashing.

More damaging to Vancouver was the return of Midshipman Pitt, now Lord Camelford. His hatred of Vancouver had festered after he had been sent back and when he returned to Britain he pursued his victim remorselessly, challenging him to a duel and once actually trying to thrash Vancouver in public. The political caricaturist James Gillray published a print of 'The Caneing in Conduit Street' which shows a heroic Pitt raising his stick to a fat and cowardly Vancouver hiding behind his brother and standing in front of 'The South Sea Fur Warehouse' advertising 'Fine Black Otter Skins' – a reference to his trading activities. On Vancouver's back is a feather cloak bearing the label, 'The Present from the King of Owyhee to George III forgot to be delivered', referring to another scurrilous story. The savage cartoon showed the extent to which many of the less savoury events on the voyage had become common currency in

113

London, where the stories of a hard, vindictive and bullying captain in the Pacific seemed all too familiar after the trial of the *Bounty* mutineers.

It is hard to say what effect the Camelford affair and Banks's lobbying actually had on Vancouver professionally, but while the Admiralty accorded him the honour of promoting all those he recommended – and he was generous in his recommendations – he was certainly beset with a number of official irritations, obstructions and delays. These were to an extent the normal workings of a bureaucracy, experienced before and since by many returning commanders, but in a letter to Lord Chatham Vancouver complained that since his return he felt 'as it were insulated, from all connections with persons of consequence' who would normally have been willing to help to resolve the issues. Vancouver was up against the Establishment, but it must have been particularly distressing to him when his oldest and most trusted colleague, Joseph Whidbey, was recruited by Banks to support the criticism of his style of command. Conspiracy theorists will note that Banks later proposed Whidbey as a Fellow of the Royal Society.

In the few years left to him Vancouver worked on writing his account of the voyage. That he was able to do so at all bearing in mind his failing health and other problems bears no small testimony to the powers of determination and concentration that made him such a good, if demanding, surveyor. Vancouver died in May 1798. For the last few months he did not have the strength to write so his brother John completed the last pages of *A Voyage of Discovery*, which was published posthumously later that year. It was reviewed favourably in the *Naval Chronicle* as a 'naval classic', although Midshipman Barrie probably reflected a general reader's response when he complained to his mother that 'I think it is one of the most tedious books I ever read'. In the Hakluyt edition of *A Voyage of Discovery* (1986), the editor, W. Kaye Lamb, wisely left the last word of his comprehensive introduction to one of Vancouver's harshest critics, Archibald Menzies, who said in his eightieth year: 'those books that Vancouver wrote – strange that he could put so much of himself into the printed page. He was a great Captain.'

Discovery as a prison hulk on the Thames; watercolour by Thomas Hosmer Shepherd, *c*.1830. Shepherd was one of a family of artists specializing in drawing London scenes. *Discovery* was converted into a bomb vessel after Vancouver's voyage, becoming a prison hulk in 1808 before being finally broken up in 1834.

CHAPTER SEVEN

'AN HERCULEAN LABOUR': MATTHEW FLINDERS' CIRCUMNAVIGATION OF AUSTRALIA

'I have ten-thousand difficulties and dangers
to encounter. I have undertaken an Herculean labour.'
– *Matthew Flinders*

*I*n the autumn of 1800 a young naval lieutenant newly arrived back in Britain wrote an excited letter to his future wife. In it he described his arrival at what he saw as a turning point in his life:

> You see that I make everything subservient to business. Indeed
> my dearest friend, this time seems to be a very critical period of
> my life. I have been long absent, – have done services abroad that
> were not expected, but which seem to be thought a good deal of.
> I have more and greater friends than before, and this seems to be
> the moment that their exertions may be most serviceable to me. I
> may now perhaps make a bold dash forward, or may remain a
> poor lieutenant all my life.

The young lieutenant's name was Matthew Flinders, his future wife was his childhood friend Ann Chappelle and the 'services abroad' were a series of charts he had made of Australia with his colleague, the naval surgeon George Bass. In a succession of boats, the smallest of which had been an 8-foot dinghy called *Tom Thumb*, the two men had started to survey the coast on either side of Port Jackson, but the feat which got them really noticed was the circumnavigation of Van Diemen's Land (Tasmania), which proved it was an island and established, in the Bass Strait, a much shorter route for ships sailing the southern route from the Cape of Good Hope to Sydney.

Flinders had sailed as a midshipman on William Bligh's second breadfruit voyage to Tahiti and the West Indies (1791–93). Although he and Bligh fell out, Flinders managed to pick up three things on the

Matthew Flinders (1774–1814),
from an autograph copy of his
parole after six years in captivity
on Ile de France (Mauritius).

Providence, all of which were to affect him in later life: the basics of
marine surveying, venereal disease and an appreciation of the influence
that Sir Joseph Banks had in all matters to do with exploration. On his
return from Australia in 1800, where his ship *Reliance* had been stationed
for nearly four years, Flinders shrewdly dedicated his charts to Banks –
surely the most important of the new and great friends he mentions – and
sent him an ambitious plan for a complete survey of the coast of Australia.

Very little more had been learnt about Australia's shores since Cook's
running survey of the east coast, while, as Flinders himself put it, 'the vast
interior of this new continent was wrapped in total obscurity'. Flinders
proposed a full scientific expedition to survey the entire coast for possible
harbours and rivers, while an onboard party of scientists and artists would
explore the land's natural resources. This was to be scientific exploration in
the style of Cook, although with a more openly colonial purpose.

Two years earlier, Banks had had a similar plan turned down by an

Admiralty understandably preoccupied by the war at sea; but, nothing daunted, he endorsed Flinders' plan and sent it off again, and this time it was accepted. What caused the change of heart was that the French government had just requested a passport guaranteeing safe passage for a scientific voyage to Australia under the command of Nicolas Baudin. Although the subsequent history of Flinders' voyage would show only too well that the gentlemanly scientific ideals of the Enlightenment were coming under pressure after years of war, the Admiralty had very little choice but to grant Baudin a passport. But neither were they blind to the potential embarrassment of France exploring and naming what was, arguably at least, a British possession. In reality, the Admiralty had very little strategic interest in Australia at that time but they had no intention of being beaten by the French in any aspect of maritime activity.

The ship selected was a north-country collier, originally built as the *Fram* but then bought by the Navy, converted into a sloop-of-war and renamed *Xenophon*. This followed Cook's famous choice of roomy, sturdy and round-bottomed colliers for long voyages of exploration; but *Xenophon*'s structure had been strained by the original conversion and the ship leaked badly from the first – a weakness that would eventually have disastrous effects on the voyage. It was, wrote Flinders, choosing his words carefully some years later, 'the best vessel which could, at that time, be

Admiralty plan of *Investigator*'s quarterdeck showing the 'plant cabbin' that Sir Joseph Banks had ordered to be taken out to Australia and erected in Port Jackson. It was designed to hold the live plants he hoped his naturalists would collect.

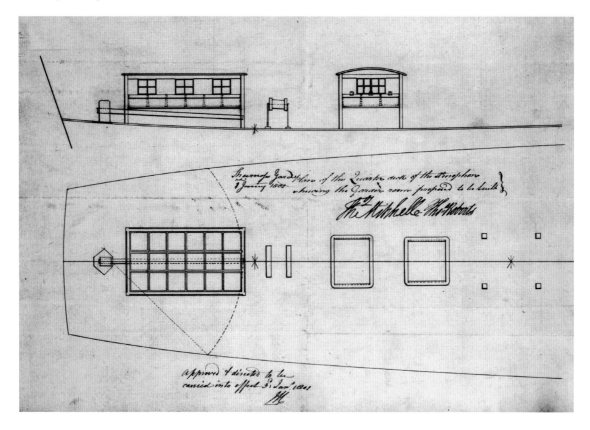

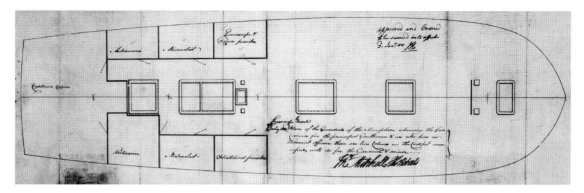

Admiralty deck plan showing the cabin layout of *Investigator.*

spared for the projected voyage'. Neither he nor Banks felt inclined to risk the abandonment of the voyage by pushing for a better ship and so *Xenophon* was renamed once again, this time as *Investigator.* Flinders was appointed its captain and, in February 1801, promoted to the rank of commander. The hope that he had expressed in his letter to Ann Chappelle had been realized: he would now no longer stay a 'poor lieutenant' for the rest of his days.

The Admiralty gave Banks virtually a free hand to plan the voyage and select the scientific personnel, telling him that 'any proposal you may make will be approved, the whole is left entirely to your decision'. For the all-important post of naturalist, Banks turned once again to Scotland, appointing a graduate of Edinburgh University named Robert Brown, who was to be assisted by a gardener, Peter Good. There were to be two artists: Ferdinand Bauer, responsible for the 'natural history' – the plants, animals and fish collected on the voyage – and a young man named William Westall as the landscape painter. In addition there was to be a mineralogist and an astronomer, although the latter, John Crossley, left the ship at Cape Town because of illness and his role would be filled for the rest of the voyage by Flinders and his brother Samuel, who had been appointed as one of the *Investigator*'s lieutenants.

Banks made sure that the ship was supplied with the finest scientific equipment, personally sent a set of the *Encyclopaedia Britannica* on board and arranged for the East India Company, which had some interest in the outcomes of the voyage, to give Flinders and his officers 'table money'. The Board of Longitude equipped *Investigator* with astronomical instruments and chronometers, including K3 (Larcum Kendall's third chronometer) which had accompanied Vancouver to the Pacific in 1791. For Banks as well as Flinders this was undoubtedly conceived of as a voyage of scientific exploration in the manner and spirit of Cook. Its scale suggests that in some ways Banks saw it as the one he had planned but finally withdrawn from on Cook's *Resolution* in 1772.

Flinders busied himself preparing his ship for its long voyage. When he had a problem he applied to Banks first, who generally managed to fix it. Flinders, conscious and proud that he was the second generation of Cook's lieutenants, followed the great navigator's advice on scurvy by loading anti-scorbutics such as sauerkraut and malt extract, insisting that each man drank a pint of this 'wort' every day. The Navy had adopted lemon juice as the most effective countermeasure for the disease in 1796 and, while Flinders' use of ineffective anti-scorbutics may have shown admirable loyalty to the memory of Cook, his reliance on them was destined to cost him dear during the voyage. The Admiralty received a passport from the French guaranteeing *Investigator* safe passage and by June 1801 the ship was ready, *The Times* reporting that 'she is admirably fitted out for the intended service, and is manned with picked men, who are distinguished by a glazed hat decorated with a globe, and the name of the ship in letters of gold'. One sees the purse of Banks rather than the hand of Flinders behind this delightful bit of theatre.

Achromatic telescope by J. Dolland of London, belonging to Matthew Flinders.

Alongside the public preparations for the voyage, which can be traced through Flinders' journal, his book (*A Voyage to Terra Australis*, 1814), and official documents in British and Australian archives, a personal drama was unfolding. Flinders was a prolific, entertaining and revealing letter writer and his letters to Ann Chappelle offer a rare glimpse of the personal problems that must have hovered behind many such voyages. Ann was clearly very attracted to Flinders and had agreed to marry him, but once she realized that his plans for the immediate future involved him returning to Australia for another three or four years she cooled noticeably. Flinders visited her in Lincolnshire at Christmas 1800 and the visit was not a success: 'Thou didst not just return me answers to questions put', he wrote as soon as he got back to London, 'thou offered nothing for me to consider. Thou asked me no question. Thou seemed to wish no conversation upon the subject that I was so interested about … tears are in my eyes – I am torn to pieces.'

At the Christmas meeting Ann gave Matthew 'Pleasures of Memory', probably an edition of Samuel Rogers' well-known poem of that title (1792), and both of them seem to have considered the relationship at an end, although they continued to correspond. Flinders' letters between January and April 1801 have not survived. In April 1801, however, he came up with a bright idea:

> Thou has asked me if there is a *possibility* of our living together. I think I see a *probability* of our living with a moderate share of comfort. Till now I was not certain of being able to fit myself out clear of the world. I have now done it, and have accommodation on board the *Investigator*, in which as my wife a woman may, with love to assist her, make herself happy.
>
> It will be much better to keep this matter entirely secret. There are many reasons for it, and I have also a powerful one. I do not know how my great friends might like it.

Flinders had changed the cabin layout in the *Investigator* to create a small private bedroom off the great cabin and his plan was that Ann would sail with him to Port Jackson where she would be able to live relatively cheaply and see her husband whenever the ship returned there to refit. Flinders was right in thinking that this should be kept 'entirely secret'. Sir Joseph Banks was no romantic, thundering some years later when hearing of the marriage of one of his Australian plant collectors, and probably thinking of Flinders, that 'this marrying has often been in my way ... I did not hire him to beget a family in N.S. Wales'. Flinders and Ann duly married but Banks heard of it when he, a Lincolnshire man like Flinders, was sent a local paper. By ill chance, the new First Lord of the Admiralty, Earl St Vincent, also paid *Investigator* an unscheduled visit and was surprised to find the captain's wife on board, and obviously not simply visiting. No official decision had been made on Ann when *Investigator* left Sheerness at the end of May and began to work its way down the English Channel with her still on board. Bad luck struck again when *Investigator* ran aground off Dungeness while captain and wife were below and at this point Flinders was in real danger of losing his job. Although Banks was furious that Flinders had put him in an embarrassing situation, he did not want the voyage compromised before it had even started and so did his best to ease the situation. Flinders kept his command, although he never again really had the full trust of the Admiralty, and Ann was packed off to live with her family, leaving as a memento of her time on *Investigator* a few words, which the couple referred to as her 'forget me not', pencilled on their cabin wall. They were not to see each other for more than nine years.

The incident throws some aspects of Flinders' character into sharp relief. When faced with a choice between marriage or exploration he chose the latter, which suggests, incorrectly, that he felt a burning desire to be an explorer. He was indeed an intensely ambitious man but he saw a career in the Navy entirely pragmatically: 'Sea; I am thy servant', he once wrote, 'but thy wages must afford me more than a bare subsistence.' Money was always important to Flinders: exploration gave him the chance to stand out from the mass of other unconnected and unknown lieutenants, but more importantly to make his fortune. He calculated that the voyage would earn him the substantial sum of £1500 from wages and the publication of the official narrative and charts. Flinders was a very intelligent man, but one who knew it all too well. His confidence in his own abilities led him to take risks which made him an effective explorer but also on occasion led him into extremely dangerous situations, for his self-confidence could seamlessly blend into an arrogant conviction that he could get away with anything. He probably left Britain feeling elated that he had managed to marry Ann and still keep command of the voyage, rather than concerned that he had lost the trust of Banks and the Admiralty and, temporarily at least, embittered his wife.

Ann resented the forced separation deeply and her first letters to him, which he received more than a year later, were clearly cudgelling him for following the 'call of his profession' and showing 'poor proof' of his love for her. Flinders, for his part, simply missed their brief period of intimacy:

> Oh, write to me constantly [he wrote from Cape Town in November 1801], write me pages and volumes. Tell me the dress thou wearest, and at what time in the morning thou puttest on thy stockings; tell me thy dreams, – any thing: so do but talk to me, and of thyself. When thou art sitting at thy kneedle [*sic*] and alone, then think on me, my love; and write me the uppermost of thy thoughts. Fill me half a dozen sheets and send them when thou canst.

After a stop at Cape Town where the ship was recaulked to try to stop a worrying leak that had first made its appearance in the English Channel, *Investigator* made a landfall at Vancouver's old anchorage in 'King George the Third's Sound' on the south-west tip of Australia, after a passage of just under five months. Flinders' Instructions allowed him to stop here briefly for water but then ordered him to hurry on to Port Jackson for refitting before commencing the survey. The Admiralty had divided the mammoth task of charting Australia's 30,000-kilometre coastline into sections and gave Flinders unambiguous instructions on the order in which he was to complete them, according to navigational, scientific and

Chart of part of the south coast of Australia. From *A Voyage to Terra Australis*, by Matthew Flinders. The chart shows clearly the dangers of the coast and the *Investigator*'s track through the hazards.

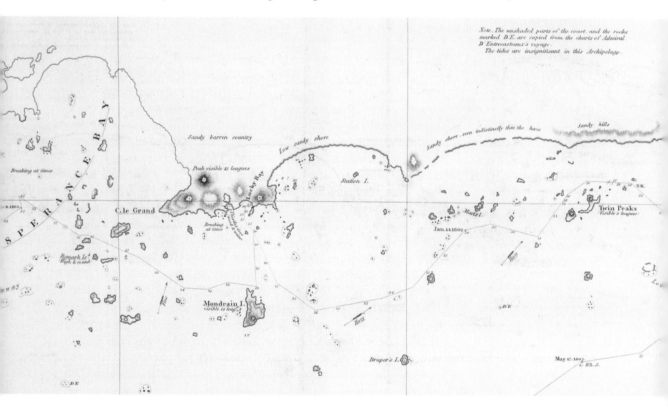

King George's Sound, by William Westall. The *Investigator* stayed in the sound from 9 December 1801 to 5 January 1802. Westall felt that Australia offered him little of the exotic scenery that he had hoped would make his reputation within the artistic establishment. Although the expedition had its only sustained contact with Aborigines at King George's Sound, Westall's representation of both them and the Australian landscape was heavily romanticized.

political priorities. Typically, Flinders promptly ignored the orders and spent some weeks in the sound (now the site of the city of Albany) refitting *Investigator* and resurveying the harbour before starting his survey of the south coast of Australia on the way to Port Jackson.

The southern route was the quickest for ships sailing to Port Jackson from Cape Town, but they sailed well south of the coast itself, usually making their landfall on Tasmania. Bruny D'Entrecasteaux had surveyed parts of the coast in his search for Lapérouse in 1791–93, but a full and accurate chart was long overdue. There would be obvious advantages for colonial development if Flinders were able to discover useable rivers and harbours along this stretch. There was also a persuasive but incorrect geographical theory that *Terra Australis* was not one single continent but two, split in half by a waterway stretching from the Gulf of Carpentaria in the north to the south coast, and Flinders had orders to search for it. In addition, he was acutely aware that Nicolas Baudin's expedition had set off before him and Flinders was anxious to claim the honour of being the first to survey and name this jewel in the crown of Australian marine surveying.

There was nothing fundamentally wrong with Flinders' decision to survey the south coast immediately: the Admiralty had made it his number one task anyway and, as Flinders pointed out in his published account, he was going to have to follow it to get to Port Jackson and so it made sense to survey as he went along. The real problem was that instead of exploring during the cooler months, as in the original plan, it was actually done at the height of summer, when the blistering heat created an arid desert where the botanists had hoped to find new and exotic plants. The naturalist Robert Brown always felt bitter about Flinders' decision and complained about it to Banks, noting in addition that Flinders gave the scientists few opportunities to go ashore. Banks, however, backed the captain, telling Brown that he did not know how lucky he was: 'Had Cooke [*sic*] paid the same attention to the naturalists as he [Flinders] seems to have done we should have done much more [on the *Endeavour* voyage].'

By the end of February 1802 Flinders had surveyed most of the Great Australian Bight, that enormous, curved coastline stretching from the south-west tip of Australia to the approaches to the Bass Strait. It was here, at a place that Flinders named Cape Catastrophe, that tragedy struck. 'It will grieve thee, as it has me', he wrote to Ann, who of course knew the *Investigator*'s crew personally, 'that poor Thistle was lost upon the south coast.' John Thistle was the ship's master and had sailed with Flinders for some years. 'Thou knowest how I valued him', Flinders continued, but:

> he is however gone, as well as Mr Taylor and six seamen, who were all drowned in a boat. No remains of them were found; but the boat, which was stove all to pieces against the rocks, was picked up.

Flinders described in *A Voyage to Terra Australis* how 'he caused an inscription to be engraven upon a sheet of copper and set up on a stout post' in Memory Cove, the little bay where the boat was found, while the names of the drowned men – Thistle, Taylor, Little, Lewis, Hopkins, Smith, Williams and Grindal – were remembered in nearby islands which still bear their names today.

Little more than a month after the tragedy, the expedition met Baudin's ship, *Géographe* (which had become separated from its consort, *Naturaliste*) surveying the coast from east to west. Curiously, Flinders makes no mention of the meeting at Encounter Bay in his letters to Ann but describes it fully in his book. The two ships approached each other cautiously, Flinders recording that 'we veered round as *Le Géographe* was passing, so as to keep our broadside to her, lest the flag of truce should be a deception', before being rowed over to the French ship with Robert Brown who, unlike Flinders, spoke good French. The ships stayed in company for two days and the meeting was courteous, if a little strained. According to Flinders he first asked to see Baudin's passport and 'when it was found and I had perused it, [I] offered him mine from the French marine minister, but he put it back without inspection'. Unusually, Flinders' passport was made out in the name of the ship, not its captain, and while this minor detail was either not noticed or not remarked on by Baudin or Brown it would play a significant role in the last part of the voyage.

After exchanging information on their surveys the two ships parted, *Géographe* to continue west for a while and *Investigator* to complete the survey of the Bass Strait and then head for Port Jackson. Flinders arrived there on 9 May 1802 and immediately began the process of refitting and reprovisioning his ship, although finding time to write proudly to Ann in 'a moment snatched from the confusion of performing half a dozen occupations' that they had:

A Bay on the South Coast of Australia, by William Westall. The survey of the south coast took the *Investigator* through the dangerous Recherche Archipelago. One evening they were surrounded by a 'labyrinth of islands and rocks' which seemed to offer neither passage out to open water nor shelter. Flinders made boldly for the coast, finding a small sandy bay where they thankfully dropped anchor for the night. They called this Lucky Bay and stayed on for some days to explore the area.

> done much towards the accomplishment of the service for which we came out … Had we found an inlet which would admit us into the interior of New Holland, I should have been better pleased, but as such did not exist, we could not find it; several important discoveries however are made, of islands, bays and inlets; of these, when the charts go home thou wilt probably see something said in the newspapers.

He also brought her up to date on the ship's news, telling her of his improving relationship with his first lieutenant, Robert Fowler; the growing distance between him and his brother Samuel, who 'is satisfied with being as much inferior to other officers as I would have him superior to them'; the impressive ability of his kinsman, the young midshipman John Franklin (the future governor of Tasmania and Arctic explorer, who would die looking for the North-West Passage), who 'is capable of

learning every thing that we can shew him'; and the robust health of his cat, Trim, named after the faithful servant Corporal Trim, a character in Laurence Sterne's novel *Tristram Shandy*.

A month later, in July 1802, Flinders received two letters from Ann, only six and nine months after they had been written. A further two letters predating them failed to arrive. In them Ann complained about his abandonment of her and while he made no apologies for his decision to go to Australia, he reassured her eloquently of his love, telling her again that the survey would make their fortunes and urging her 'to submit to what has been decreed for us, and look forward with our best hopes for the good which is in store for us'. He also had to give her the news that:

> I had desired Elder [his servant] to scrub out the little
> cabin, and to scour the paintwork; – this was done, and
> when afterwards I looked for thy *forget me not*, to indulge
> myself with fond thoughts of thee, – it was not to be found
> … I sighed myself to sleep and dreamed of thee; and
> although it is now sometime since, I am not reconciled. I
> thought of tracing them again, but it would not be thy
> writing, and unless it was so, it was nothing; the sentence,
> however, is so engraven on my memory, that the place where
> it was written brings every letter of it to my recollection,
> even to the cross on the T, at the end of *not*.

Flinders ended by telling Ann that he would not be able to hear from her again for at least a year as *Investigator* was about to embark on the second phase of the voyage – the survey of the north-east coast, the Torres Strait, the Gulf of Carpentaria and north Australia. Flinders, typically, interpreted his instructions freely and began with a section of the east coast that he had been expressly ordered to leave to the last. *Investigator* was to be accompanied by the brig *Lady Nelson*, which boasted an innovative sliding keel designed by Captain John Schanck for navigation in shallow waters. Unfortunately the design did not work, *Lady Nelson* became more a liability than a help and Flinders eventually sent her back to Port Jackson. Flinders also took with him an old companion from an early Australian voyage, a man called, in Flinders' spelling, Bongaree, one of the Eora tribe, which lived in the Port Jackson area. While his use as an interpreter had been limited, as different tribes spoke very different languages, Flinders had found him very useful in establishing and mediating contact with Aboriginal peoples and had no hesitation in employing this 'worthy and brave fellow' again.

Flinders sailed the *Investigator* up the east coast, following Cook's route between the Great Barrier Reef and the open ocean and missing, as Cook had done before him, the eight rivers that empty into the sea along a 200-mile stretch of New South Wales, today called the Northern Rivers District. The governor of Port Jackson, Phillip Gidley King, asked

Flinders to survey the section between Cape Tribulation, where the *Endeavour* had nearly been lost, and the Torres Strait in order to find a passage through what Cook had called 'The Labyrinth'. It would have been an important discovery, as ships heading up or down the east coast of Australia usually made a wide detour around the coast of New Guinea in order to avoid the dual dangers of the reef and strait. Although Flinders did find a route through the Great Barrier Reef, later named the Flinders Passage, he had left the coast too far to the south for it to serve King's purpose and The Labyrinth would eventually be surveyed by his son, Phillip Parker King, in the *Mermaid* in 1819 (who would also be accompanied by Flinders' Aborigine companion, Bongaree).

Because Flinders had been delayed on the east coast and was consequently worried about being caught by the approaching monsoon, his survey of the Torres Strait was far from adequate. More worrying for him was the reappearance of the *Investigator*'s leak, which was soon running at the rate of twelve inches an hour. Nevertheless, Flinders continued to follow the north coast of Australia, surveying the Gulf of Carpentaria and Arnhem Land, which were known at that time only through the inaccurate seventeenth-century charts of Dutch navigators. Some of Flinders' surveys of the gulf were still in use during the Second World War, although this was less because of their quality than that the swampy and remote area had not merited more accurate charting in the intervening years.

By the following June, *Investigator* was back in Port Jackson. The leak had worsened and while on the north coast Flinders ordered a survey of the ship which, he later wrote to Ann, 'proves her to be so very much decayed as to be totally irrepairable [*sic*]. It was the unanimous opinion of the surveying officers that had we met a severe gale of wind in the passage from Timor, that she must have been crushed like an egg'. Flinders abandoned his cartographic survey and sailed back via Timor and the west coast of Australia, so becoming the first to circumnavigate the continent. The poor state of the ship was matched by that of the crew, which was badly hit by disease caught in Timor as well as by scurvy: 'Douglas – the boatswain, is gone, – the sergeant, two quarter masters and another followed before we got into this port; and since, the gardener and three others are laid in earth.' The cat Trim, he reported, 'like his master is becoming grey', for Flinders had also suffered during the voyage from scurvy and lameness, the latter caused by 'the gravelly', the kidney complaint which made urination painful and which was eventually to kill him at the age of forty. Modern medical opinion is that Flinders' 'gravelly' was a long-term effect of the gonorrhoea he had contracted in Tahiti as a young man, or more probably of the surgeon's treatment of the disease, which consisted of cleansing the urinary passage with a solution of mercury nitrate.

Flinders began this letter to his wife in Port Jackson but it was finished and finally posted in Ile de France (Mauritius). Once *Investigator* had been condemned as irreparable in Port Jackson, Governor King gave Flinders and the majority of his crew permission to sail back to Britain on a ship called the *Porpoise*. However, he gave Flinders' first lieutenant, Robert Fowler, the command, so leaving Flinders free to complete his charts during the voyage. They sailed in company with two other ships, *Bridgewater* and *Cato*. Seven hundred miles north of Port Jackson, *Porpoise* and *Cato* struck a reef and were lost – the *Bridgewater* sailed on, knowingly leaving the shipwrecked crews to their fate. After transferring as much of the *Porpoise*'s stores ashore as possible, together with his valuable manuscript charts, Flinders and thirteen others set off for Port Jackson in the ship's cutter, christened *Hope* for the occasion. Thirteen days later he brought the small open boat into Port Jackson where King gave him command of yet another vessel, the 29-ton colonial schooner *Cumberland*, and sent him back to pick up the survivors. They were accompanied by the East Indiaman *Rolla*, which was contracted to take the majority of the crew back to Britain via Canton, while Flinders was to sail directly home on the schooner with a small crew.

On 11 October Flinders left the *Rolla* at Wreck Reef and set sail for the Torres Strait and then for Cape Town in a ship that was really designed for short coastal voyages. *Cumberland* was small, wet and cramped – Flinders described filling in his daily journal in her as being like trying to write while riding a horse in a thunderstorm. She also leaked badly and became unsafe when one of the two pumps, which together had barely kept ahead of the leaks, broke down in the Indian Ocean. Flinders

View of Sir Edward Pellew's Group, Northern Territory, December 1802, by William Westall.

felt he had no choice but to put into Ile de France and rely on his passport from the French government either to permit him to make repairs to the *Cumberland* or negotiate a passage home on a bigger ship. Much to his surprise and outrage it soon became clear that he was not to be treated as a distinguished scientific officer and honoured guest but rather that the governor, General Decaen, suspected him of being a spy. Flinders made the situation worse by deliberately insulting Decaen, not removing his hat in his presence and archly turning down an invitation to a dinner that was probably being offered as an olive branch.

Flinders was to remain a prisoner on Ile de France for six years, despite a number of formal and informal requests for his release. The imprisonment was not altogether unpleasant as he was eventually permitted to stay in the country with the d'Arifat family and he made a number of close and lasting friends among the island's upper classes, many of whom were royalists and as opposed to the Bonapartist government of Decaen as was Flinders. But to a man of Flinders' energy and ambition any imprisonment was torture: ' "I can't get out!" cried the starling. "God help thee," says Yorick, "but I'll let thee out" ', he wrote to Ann, quoting again from Laurence Sterne and expressing his sense of helplessness. Flinders probably feared anonymity more than anything and when he did finally return home in 1810 it must have been obvious to him that during

Wreck Reef, by William Westall. The uncharted reef where *Porpoise* was lost on 17 August 1803 was sketched at the time and later painted by William Westall. It was one of the few Australian scenes to which he would return repeatedly and he was working on another version of it when he died.

the long imprisonment his voyage had faded from both the public's and the Admiralty's minds. Worse, perhaps, was that the narrative and charts from Baudin's voyage had already been published while he was imprisoned (although Baudin himself had died on Ile de France only weeks before Flinders' arrival) and Flinders was furious to see that the names Terre Napoléon, Golfe Bonaparte and Golfe Joséphine appeared on coasts he had originally charted and named: 'not even the smallest island [was] left without some similar stamp of French discovery . . .'

The long separation was also difficult for Ann, who at one stage appeared to be prepared to join Flinders on Ile de France. She also had to cope with his airy and somewhat insensitive descriptions of his friendships with the pretty daughters of Mme d'Arifat – 'I am not one of those suspicious husbands that think their wives are necessarily doing wrong whenever they have anything they desire to keep to themselves', he said in what was possibly a veiled suggestion that Ann should not be suspicious of him. Some believe that Flinders did have an affair with Delphine d'Arifat, and even that she had his child; but while a flirtation is possible, even probable, there is absolutely no evidence of an affair and his letters to Ann are consistent in their expressions of love:

> I am as it were shut up in a cask that has been rolled with violence from the top of hope down into the vale of misfortune; I am bruised and well nigh stunned out of my senses; but canst thou imagine the addition it would be to this misery for the cask to have been driven full of spike nails; – such is the increase of misery to my feelings on thinking intensely on thee.

Ann saw her husband again on 25 October 1810, nine and a half years since they had parted. John Franklin witnessed their meeting but, feeling 'so sensibly the affecting scene of your meeting Mrs Flinders that I could not have remained any longer in the room under any consideration', he tactfully slipped out of the door. The remaining four years of Flinders' life were spent in preparing his charts and book for publication: he died on the day the first copies came off the press.

The *Investigator*'s had been the best-equipped British voyage of scientific exploration since Cook's. It had some great successes: the voyage's natural history was outstanding, a contemporary botanist writing that 'the specimens, the descriptions & drawings brought home from New Holland by Brown & Bauer, are by far the most excellent that ever resulted from any expedition'. Flinders' surveys were often of a high order, but the ambitious programme gave him little time to do more than trace the outlines of the coast and he has frequently, if rather unfairly, been criticized for missing important rivers and harbours. Flinders brought many of his problems on

Pencil sketch of a waterfall in Mauritius, a noted local beauty spot. This is among Flinders' papers but the artist has not yet been identified.

Phyllopteryx taeniolatus (Weedy Seadragon), by Ferdinand Bauer.

himself: altering the order of the surveys had a far greater impact on the voyage than he could have realized, while 'playing free with the land', as he described his determination to ensure accuracy by following the coast as close inshore as possible, led to the repeated groundings that materially weakened the already strained structure of the *Investigator* and contributed to the vessel's eventual abandonment, and so to the premature end to the survey. His arrogant attitude to General Decaen was undoubtedly the cause of his extended imprisonment, and this effectively meant that the narrative and charts of the voyage did not appear until 1814, when the *Investigator* and its commander had long faded from the public memory.

Flinders has remained a little-known name in the history of British maritime exploration since that time, but he has long been acknowledged in Australia as one of the key figures in its early colonial history, and rightly so. He is widely believed to have been the first to use the word 'Australia' in print, although sadly for history that distinction actually belonged to the less well-known George Shaw, who referred to the 'vast Island or rather Continent of Australia, Australasia, or New Holland' in his 1794 book, *Zoology of New Holland*. But Flinders did use 'Australia' both in the text and general chart of his *Voyage to Terra Australis*, against the strong preference of Sir Joseph Banks, and it was Flinders' use of it that saw the name generally accepted some years after his death.

General chart of Australia, from *A Voyage to Terra Australis*, by Matthew Flinders. It shows his great improvements of accuracy, most notably that Tasmania is a separate island, not the peninsula shown in earlier charts.

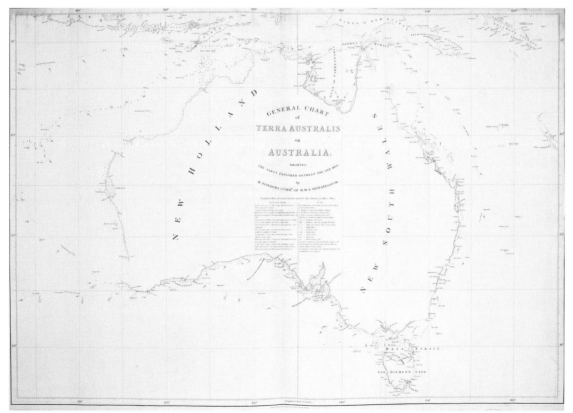

Year	1776	1778	1779	1780
General	July: Cook sails on his last voyage in *Resolution* and *Discovery*. American War of Independence begins	France allies with American rebels	14 Feb.: Cook killed on Hawaii. Spain enters war as ally of American rebels	Cook's ships return home. Holland enters war as ally of American rebels
Arthur Phillip (b. 1738)	In Portuguese service in Brazil (from 1775)	Sept.: returns to England	Promoted commander	
Jean-François de Galaup de Lapérouse (b. 1741)		Appointed command 14-gun corvette *Serin*. May: given command of new frigate, *Amazone*	Captures British frigate off the American coast	Takes command of the frigate *Astrée*
William Bligh (b. 1754)	Master of Cook's *Resolution*			
Alejandro Malaspina (b. 1754)	In Spanish navy since 1774	Promoted frigate lieutenant		In 'Moonlight Action' off Cape St Vincent (Spanish v British)
George Vancouver (b. 1757)	Midshipman in *Discovery* under Captain Charles Clerke on Cook's last voyage			Promoted lieutenant in *Martin* on return of *Discovery*
Matthew Flinders (b. 1774)				

1781	1782	1783	1784	1785
Aug.: Battle of Dogger Bank (British v Dutch)		American War of Independence ends	Publication of official account of Cook's last voyage	First British fur-trading ship reaches NW coast of America from India
Promoted captain in *Ariadne*		Commands *Europe* to India via Rio de Janeiro and Cape Town	April: returns to England then leaves for France	Oct.: returns, then back to France again
	Takes command of 74-gun *Sceptre* and leads expedition to attack Hudson's Bay Company trading posts			Appointed to lead voyage of exploration to the Pacific in *Boussole* and *Astrolabe* (de Langle). 1 Aug.: leaves Brest
Marries. Master of *Belle Poule*, including at Battle of Dogger Bank. Promoted lieutenant	Serves at relief of Gibraltar	Commands merchant ships for wife's uncle until 1787		
	Serves in siege of Gibraltar; promoted frigate captain			
	Martin joins West Indies Squadron			

YEAR	1786	1787	1788	1789
General	Six more British fur-trading ships reach NW American coast from Britain and India		John Meares leads fur-trading voyage to NW American coast	June. British fur-trading vessels seized by Spanish at Nootka Sound. July: French Revolution begins
Arthur Phillip (b. 1738)	Aug.: appointed First Fleet commander and governor of NSW	13 May: sails in *Sirius* with First Fleet, via Rio and Cape Town	20 Jan.: fleet arrives at Botany Bay. 26 Jan.: moves to Port Jackson (Sydney)	Feb.: Norfolk Island settled. May: *Sirius* resupplies Port Jackson from Cape Town
Jean-François de Galaup de Lapérouse (b. 1741)	Enters Pacific via Cape Horn. April: reaches Easter Island. May: reaches Hawaii. June: begins survey of NW American coast. Sept.: visits Spanish settlement at Monterey	1 Jan.: reaches Macao. Surveys NE Asian coast as far as Kamchatka. Dec.: ships' boats attacked in Samoa	26 Jan.: arrives Botany Bay. 10 March: leaves Botany Bay and disappears. Both ships wrecked on Vanikoro in the Santa Cruz group, but fate not discovered until 1827.	
William Bligh (b. 1754)		23 Dec.: *Bounty* sails on breadfruit voyage to Tahiti	March: turns back from Cape Horn to Cape Town. 26 Oct.: reaches Tahiti 'east-about'	4 March: sails for East Indies. 28 April: cast adrift after *Bounty* mutiny off Tofoa, Tonga. 14 June: reaches Timor
Alejandro Malaspina (b. 1754)	Commands *Astrea* and sails round the world on behalf of Royal Philippines Company		Returns from circum-navigation. Sept.: plan for comprehensive survey voyage approved	July: sails from Cadiz with *Descubierta* and *Atrevida* (José Bustamante). Survey from Montevideo south round Cape Horn
George Vancouver (b. 1757)	Third lieutenant in *Europa*, West Indies Squadron. Surveys West Indian harbours		Appointed first lieutenant, *Europa*	Sept.: *Europa* paid off
Matthew Flinders (b. 1774)				

1790	1791	1792	1793	1794
Bounty burnt at Pitcairn Island by mutineers under Christian. British fleet mobilized as result of Nootka Sound Incident	Captain Edwards of *Pandora* seizes *Bounty* men remaining on Tahiti. *Pandora* wrecked on Barrier Reef	Trial of surviving *Bounty* mutineers brought home by Edwards	Jan.: Louis XVI executed. French Revolutionary War between France and Britain begins	1 June. Battle of the Glorious First of June (Howe v French)
Sirius wrecked on Norfolk Island. June: Second Fleet arrives. Drought at Port Jackson	Aug. – Oct.: Third Fleet arrives. Drought at Port Jackson ends	First good harvest. Phillip leaves Sydney in December	May: arrives home	
	Search mission under Bruny D'Entrecasteaux leaves in September		D'Entrecasteaux dies	
March: returns to England. Promoted commander and captain	April: appointed commander of second breadfruit voyage in *Providence* and *Assistant*. 3 Aug.: sails via Cape Town	9 April–20 July: *Providence* and *Assistant* at Tahiti	Jan.: delivers breadfruit to West Indies via East Indies and St Helena. Aug.: arrives home	
Surveys west coast of South and Central America as far as Panama	July: following new orders, searches for 'Strait of Anian', Alaska. August: at Nootka Sound. Returns to Acapulco	Crosses North Pacific to Guam and Philippines. Bustamante visits Macao	Feb.: visits Doubtful Sound, New Zealand. Visits Port Jackson, NSW, and Vava'u, Tonga	Surveys south from Callao round South America to Falkland Islands and Montevideo. Sept.: returns to Cadiz
Jan.: appointed first lieutenant, *Discovery*. Dec.: appointed master and commander of *Discovery*	7 Jan.: *Discovery* and *Chatham* sail from Deptford bound for NW American coast. Stops briefly at and charts King George III Sound, Australia (now Albany). Dec.: reaches Tahiti	March: reaches Hawaiian islands. 17 April: makes landfall in America. Begins survey. Sept.: begins negotiations with Quadra in Nootka Sound. Visits San Francisco and Monterey	Feb.: arrives to winter in Hawaii. April: recommences survey of NW America. Sept.: abandons survey for season. Sails for Hawaii via Monterey	Hawaii 'ceded' to Britain by King Kamehameha. April: arrives Cook's River (now Cook Inlet), Alaska, for final survey season. 19 Aug.: survey completed
Appointed able seaman and later midshipman in *Bellerophon*	Joins Bligh's *Providence* as midshipman for second breadfruit voyage		7 Sept.: Rejoins *Bellerophon*	At Battle of the Glorious First of June. Joins *Reliance* as midshipman to take Governor Hunter to Port Jackson

YEAR	1795	1796	1797	1798
General	Sept.: John Hunter arrives as new governor of NSW		14 Feb.: Battle of Cape St Vincent (Jervis v Spanish). April–May: fleet mutinies at Spithead and the Nore	1 Aug.: Battle of the Nile (Nelson v French)
Arthur Phillip (b. 1738)		Returns to active service, commanding several ships, mainly in Mediterranean (–Feb. 1798)		April: commands Hampshire Sea Fencibles (–1801)
Jean-François de Galaup de Lapérouse (b. 1741)	Survivors of search mission return to France		Account of voyage published, edited by Milet-Mureau from copies of logs sent back before disappearance	
William Bligh (b. 1754)	April: takes command of *Calcutta* in North Sea	Jan.: takes command of *Director* in North Sea	11 Oct.: distinguishes himself at Battle of Camperdown (Duncan v Dutch)	
Alejandro Malaspina (b. 1754)	Promoted *brigadier* (admiral) but then tried for political conspiracy and sentenced to ten years' imprisonment			
George Vancouver (b. 1757)	12 Sept.: *Discovery* arrives at Shannon, Ireland			12 May: dies at Petersham, aged forty. His *Voyage of Discovery to the North Pacific Ocean* completed and published by his brother shortly after his death
Matthew Flinders (b. 1774)	With George Bass, explores coast south of Port Jackson in *Tom Thumb*	*Reliance* sails to Cape Town for supplies for Port Jackson	Passes examination for lieutenant in Cape Town	With Bass completes first circumnavigation of Van Diemen's Land (Tasmania) in schooner *Norfolk*

1799	1800	1801	1802	1803
	Phillip Gidley King new governor of NSW. Nicolas Baudin's expedition leaves Le Havre for Australia	2 April: Battle of Copenhagen (Nelson v Danes)	Peace of Amiens ratified, ending French Revolutionary War	Napoleonic War begins
Promoted rear-admiral		Inspector-General of Impress Service...		...and Sea Fencibles (–1805)
	Surveys Dublin and Holyhead harbours	March: commands *Glatton* and distinguishes himself at Battle of Copenhagen. May: commands *Irresistible*		Survey work in English Channel
			Account of Galiano/Valdés expedition to the Strait of Juan de Fuca (1792) published in Spain	Released from prison, exiled in Italy
Flinders surveys coast north of Port Jackson in *Norfolk*. Flinders' and Bass's charts published in London. Aug.: *Reliance* arrives back in Britain	Appointed to command *Investigator*.	Feb: Promoted commander 17 April: marries Ann Chappelle. July: sails for Australia. 9 Dec.: reaches Vancouver's old anchorage, King George's Sound.	8 April: meets French explorer Nicolas Baudin 8 May: arrives Port Jackson. 22 July: begins circumnavigation of Australia	9 June: arrives Port Jackson. Aug.: *Investigator* condemned, Flinders wrecked en route to Britain in *Porpoise*. Dec.: arrives Ile de France (Mauritius), where he is imprisoned

YEAR	1804	1805	1806	1808
General	Dec.: Napoleon crowned Emperor of the French	21 Oct.: Nelson's victory and death at Trafalgar. 2 Dec.: Napoleon victorious at Austerlitz		
Arthur Phillip (b. 1738)				Feb.: suffers stroke
Jean-François de Galaup de Lapérouse (b. 1741)				
William Bligh (b. 1754)	In Hydrographic Office. May: commands *Warrior*	April: Governor designate of NSW	Feb.: sails for Port Jackson in *Porpoise*	Jan.: deposed as governor by 'rum rebels' but refuses to leave Australia
Alejandro Malaspina (b. 1754)				
George Vancouver (b. 1757)				
Matthew Flinders (b. 1774)		Repaired and refitted *Investigator* arrives in Liverpool from Australia, carrying Robert Brown and Ferdinand Bauer.		

1809	1810	1811	1812	1814
Macquarie overthrows NSW 'rum rebellion' in December and relieves Bligh			Napoleon's retreat from Moscow	Napoleon exiled to Elba
				Promoted admiral. 31 Aug.: dies aged seventy-five
Jan.: aboard *Porpoise*, between Port Jackson and Tasmania	Jan.: Bligh returns to Sydney and home in October	Promoted rear-admiral		Promoted vice-admiral
Some astronomical observations of voyage officially published	9 April: dies in Italy aged fifty-five. First version of his journal in Spanish not published until 1885			
	May: repatriated; arrives in Britain 24 October. Promoted captain			19 July: dies aged forty. *A Voyage to Terra Australis* published same month

YEAR	1815	1817		
General	Napoleon escapes. 18 June: defeated at Waterloo. Exiled to St Helena			
Arthur Phillip (b. 1738)				
Jean-François de Galaup de Lapérouse (b. 1741)				
William Bligh (b. 1754)		7 Dec.: dies aged sixty-four		
Alejandro Malaspina (b. 1754)				
George Vancouver (b. 1757)				
Matthew Flinders (b. 1774)				

SOURCES AND FURTHER READING

Caroline Alexander, *The* Bounty*: The True Story of the Mutiny on the Bounty* (New York, 2003)

K. A. Austen, *The Voyage of the Investigator* (London, 1964)

The Britain-Australia Bicentennial Trust (publisher), *Admiral Arthur Phillip, 1738-1814* [collected annual memorial addresses, 1992-2002; London, 2002]

Daniel W. Clayton, *Islands of Truth: The Imperial Fashioning of Vancouver Island* (Vancouver, 2000)

Warren L. Cook, *Flood Tide of Empire: Spain and the Pacific Northwest, 1543–1819* (New Haven and London, 1973)

Andrew David, Felipe Fernández-Armesto, Carlos Novi, Glyndwr Williams (eds), *The Malaspina Expedition, 1789–1794: Journal of the Voyage by Alejandro Malaspina*, 3 vols (London, 2001–04)

John Dunmore, ed., *The Journal of Jean-François de Galaup de la Pérouse*, 2 vols (London, 1994)

Robin Fisher and Hugh Johnston (eds), *From Maps to Metaphors: The Pacific World of George Vancouver* (Vancouver, 1993)

Matthew Flinders, *A Voyage to Terra Australis Undertaken for the Purpose of Completing the Discovery of that Vast Country and Prosecuted in the Years 1801, 1802 and 1803* (London, 1814)

Matthew Flinders, *The Flinders Letters Online*, www.nmm.ac.uk/flinders

Alan Frost, *Arthur Phillip, 1738–1814: His Voyaging* (Melbourne, 1987)

Alan Frost, *The Global Reach of Empire: Britain's Maritime Expansion in the Indian and Pacific Oceans, 1765–1815* (Melbourne, 2003)

Barry M. Gough, *The Northwest Coast: British Navigation, Trade and Discoveries to 1812* (Vancouver, 1992)

Niel Gunson, *Messengers of Grace: Evangelical Missionaries in the South Seas, 1797–1860* (Melbourne, 1978)

Robert Hughes, *The Fatal Shore* (London, 1987)

Geoffrey Ingleton, *Matthew Flinders*, 2 vols (Guildford, 1986)

John Kendrick, *Alejandro Malaspina: Portrait of a Visionary* (Montreal, 1999)

Gavin Kennedy, *Captain Bligh: The Man and His Mutinies* (London, 1989)

Jonathan King, *The First Fleet: The Convict Voyage that Founded Australia, 1787–88* (London, 1982)

David Mabberley, *Ferdinand Bauer: The Nature of Discovery* (London, 1999)

David Mackay, *In the Wake of Cook: Exploration, Science and Empire, 1780–1801* (Beckenham, 1985)

John M. Naish, *The Interwoven Lives of George Vancouver, Archibald Menzies, Joseph Whidbey and Peter Puget: The Vancouver Voyage of 1791–1795* (Lampeter, 1996)

Richard Nokes, *Almost a Hero: The Voyages of John Meares, R.N., to China, Hawaii and the Northwest Coast* (Pullman, WA, 1998)

Arthur Phillip, *The Voyage of Governor Phillip to Botany Bay: With an Account of the Establishment of the Colonies of Port Jackson and Norfolk Island* (London, 1789 [repr. 1982])

Jonathan Raban, *Passage to Juneau: A Sea and its Meanings* (London, 1999)

Nikolai Tolstoy, *The Half-Mad Lord: Thomas Pitt, 2nd Baron Camelford* (London, 1978)

George Vancouver, *A Voyage of Discovery to the North Pacific Ocean and Round the World, 1791–1795*, W. Kaye Lamb, ed., 4 vols (London, 1984 [1798])

Glyn Williams, *Voyages of Delusion: The Search for the Northwest Passage in the Age of Reason* (London, 2002)

PICTURE ACKNOWLEDGEMENTS

National Maritime Museum, London

Images from the collection of the National Maritime Museum are listed below with their reproduction numbers and page numbers (in italics). These may be ordered by writing to the Picture Library, National Maritime Museum, Greenwich SE10 9NF or online at www.nmm.ac.uk. All images copyright © National Maritime Museum, London.

PU3304 *9*; D6607 *11*; F4140 *13*; F4142 *14* (bottom); F4143 *16–7*; D4004 *19*; BHC1035 *25*; PU2115 *32*; D7673 *38*; PU6024 *39*; PU2088 *40–1* (top); PU2980 *42*; PX7907 *44*; E3056-1 *47* (top); E3056-2 *47* (bottom); F4137 *49*; F4139 *50*; F4138 *51*; F4597 *55*; PY0750 *57*; D3970_3 (detail) *62–3*; D3970_3 (detail) *64–5*, D3970_3 (detail) *66–7*; BHC2766 *68*; B1337 *70*; PU3414 *72*; F1346 *73* (top); D3921-2 *73* (bottom); D8551-A *74* (top); D1292 *74* (bottom); E9060-1 *79*; J0509 *98*; F4836-2 *99*; BHC2576 *100*; F4151-1 *101*; F4152 *105*; D3346-2 *106* (top); F4152 *105*; F4147 *106* (bottom); PT2175 *107*; F4150 *109*; PW5976 *114–15*; PW3511 *117*; DR6224-66 *118*; DR6223-66 *119*; F4141 *120*; F4145-3 *122*; C1718 *130* (top); F4144 *131*

Greenwich Hospital Collection: BHC2959 *76*

Ministry of Defence Art Collection: BHC 4210 (detail) *1*; BHC4211 *123*; BHC4210 *125*; BHC4204 *128*; BHC1164 *129*

Illustrations are also reproduced by kind permission of the following:

Bridgeman Art Library: (Bibliothèque Mazarine, Paris) *46*; (State Library, New South Wales, Dixson Galleries) *78*

The British Library, London: *84*; *87*

Captain Cook Memorial Museum: *61*

London Missionary Society/Council for World Mission Archives, SOAS Library: *20–1*

Musée du Château de Versailles /Dagli Orti/The Art Archive: *43*

Museo de América, Madrid: *4–5*; *14* (top); *85*; *87*; *93*

Museo Naval, Madrid: *81*; *86*; *90*; *91*; *94*

Natural History Museum, London: *2–3*; *30–1*; *33*; *35*; *37*; *38–9* (top); *130* (bottom)

National Monuments Record © Crown Copyright, NMR: *24*

National Portrait Gallery, London: *23*; *59*; *97*; *113*

Royal Horticultural Society: *108*

Service historique de la marine, Vincennes: *48*; *52*

St Mary-le-Bow, Cheapside © Colin Briggs: *41*

UK Hydrographic Office: *28*; *83*; *89*

INDEX